JAPAN'S PROBLEMS

March 1954

Public Information and Cultural Affairs Bureau

Ministry of Foreign Affairs

Tokyo

159

JAPAN'S PROBLEMS

CONTENTS

This booklet is a revised reprint of a booklet with the same title, which was published by the Public Information and Cultural Affairs Bureau, Ministry of Foreign Affairs, in August 1953 for the purpose of acquainting people in foreign countries with some of the more urgent problems faced by Japan. It contains seven articles by distinguished authorities in various fields of Japan's national affairs.

JAPANESE CONSTITUTION AND
POLITICAL PARTIES

By Toshiyoshi Miyasawa

Member of the Academy of Japan

Professor of Law, Tokyo University

I

In every country where freedom of speech, press and assembly is guaranteed, political parties come into existence. In fact, the existence of political parties is "inevitable," as Bryce said, under a system of government which has been democratized in some measure.

In Japan, political parties came into existence in the Meiji Era (1868–1912) as soon as the freedom of speech, press and assembly was generally recognized. The first political party was the "Jiyu-to" (Liberal Party), established in October 1881. A year later the "Rikkenkaishin-to" (Constitutional Progressive Party) came into being. They were destined to become the two major political parties throughout the Meiji Constitution period.

The Liberal Party, asserting the sovereignty of the people, recognized the political principles embodied in the American Declaration of Independence of 1776 and the French Declaration of Human Rights of 1789.

The Constitutional Progressive Party adopted the British principle of the sovereignty of parliament and of parliamentary government.

The samurai (warrior) class which had been deprived of its privileged status as a result of the Meiji Restoration and the radical elements who were greatly dissatisfied with the Meiji regime rallied to the Liberal Party, which consequently developed a vigorous anti-Government movement. Occasionally its members resorted to brute force to achieve its aims.

The Progressive Party, however, sought a reform in government through gradual improvements.

To meet the anti-Government program of the Liberal Party, the

Meiji regime did not hesitate to resort to strong pressure. For example, it enacted the notorious Peace Preservation Regulations of 1887 and other laws restricting the freedom of political speech and of the press. As a result, the activities of the political parties were restricted, though the establishment of the Meiji Constitution later revived them.

The Meiji Constitution, the first written Constitution of Japan, was promulgated on February 11, 1889. It was established as a compromise between absolute monarchism and democracy which had assumed greater importance to the people following the Meiji Restoration. In this sense, the Constitution was patterned after the pseudo-constitutionalism of Germany.

Modelled after the various constitutions of European countries, the Meiji Constitution guaranteed freedom of speech, press and assembly. While this guarantee was by no means complete, it sufficed to establish the rights to a large extent. The Liberals and Constitutional Progressives fully utilized the new rights and through their voice in the House of Representatives began to exercise great influence over the Government.

II

The statesmen who drafted the Meiji Constitution anticipated the growth of political parties, but they had a strong aversion to allowing these parties to control the Government. However, as the House of Representatives was to be comprised of elected members, it was inevitable that political parties would come into existence and that the House would be under the control of a political group commanding a majority of the seats.

To prevent the House of Representatives from obtaining too great a power, the statesmen included in the Meiji Constitution the provision that the Imperial Diet should consist of two chambers, the House of Peers, which would be made up mainly of hereditary nobles and life members nominated by the Emperor, and the House of Representatives. The House of Peers was thus established to be a restraining force against the House of Representatives, which could be controlled by political parties.

The authors of the Constitution moreover believed that the Government should remain independent of the political parties and regarded it as undesirable for members of any political party to join the Government. Leading officials of the Government consequently considered it improper for them to have contacts with the leaders of the political parties.

However, after the Constitution came into force and the Imperial Diet began to function, the political parties, through their activities in the House of Representatives, gradually extended their influence in actual government. Under the Meiji Constitution, the concurrence of the Imperial Diet was necessary to establish laws and the national budget. Thus, a political party controlling the House of Representatives was able to block any law or budget that the Government submitted to the chamber and thus impose a check on all important actions of the Government. In this way, indirect and negative as it was, the political parties exerted a definite influence on the Government.

The political parties steadily gained in strength through the exercise of this power and began to control the Government through their action in the House of Representatives.

The Government greatly resented such activities of the political parties and even considered them to be a trespass on the prerogatives of the Emperor. Despite this antagonism, the power of the political parties grew stronger, and eventually the Government recognized the need to obtain the cooperation of the political parties in the exercise of its authority. It realized the importance of establishing close liaison with the political party controlling the House of Representatives in order to win approval of laws or the budget.

The outbreak of the Sino-Japanese War (1894–95) postponed the movement for domestic reforms as the Government and all the political parties united in the national effort to consummate the war. This experience in cooperation accelerated the development of working alliances between the Government and the political parties.

Thus was born the practice of the Government seeking the co-operation of the leading political party in the House of Representatives, and though the strength of such alliance varied there was no administration which had no ties with a political party. The strength of such cooperation gradually increased as time passed, and finally the relationship of the Government with political parties became interwoven in the model of the party cabinet of England.

Ultimately there was developed the principle that the Government depended on the confidence of the Imperial Diet, particularly the House of Representatives, and this idea was popularly called "the common way of constitutional government." In other words, it was the idea that a political party commanding the majority in the House of Representatives should hold the power of government with the party leader to be named the head of the cabinet.

This principle was materialized following the so-called " campaigns for the defense of constitutional government " in 1913 and in 1924. From 1924 to 1930 the Government of Japan was invariably a party cabinet, with the majority party in the House of Representatives, as a rule, establishing the government. However, this did not necessarily mean that such political party controlled all state affairs. The peculiarity of the Japanese Constitution withheld from the Government (or the cabinet) control of the militray forces. Matters pertaining to the army and navy were in principle outside the authority of the Government.

Though a party government in name, the Japanese Government was in reality far different from the party cabinet under the British system of government. Such party cabinets—which were actually pseudo-party cabinets—did not last long. Taking advantage of the Manchurian Incident of 1931, the military, which was outside the jurisdiction of the Government, began interfering more and more in general political matters, and eventually a militaristic fascism with the military as its main support was established.

The Government was soon controlled by the military leaders, and the Imperial Diet was relegated to the role of a rubber-stamp agency to accept the decisions of the Government. Political parties lost their voice in actual government. On the initiative of Prime Minister Prince Fumimaro Konoe, the two major political parties—" Seiyu-kai " and " Minsei-to "—and almost all the other political parties " voluntarily " dissolved themselves in 1940, and the Imperial Rule Assistance Association was established. This organization was set up with the specific purpose of assuring national cooperation with militarism and was not a genuine political party. Its formation did not mean an amalgamation of the political parties but meant their downfall.

III

The surrender of Japan to the Allied Powers in August 1945, resulted in a revolutionary change in the form of government. Japan lost her independence and became subject to the powers of the Supreme Commander for the Allied Powers under the military occupation. The Potsdam Declaration, establishing the principles of Japan's surrender and postwar policy, ordered the Japanese Government to establish freedom of speech, religion and thought and to respect the fundamental human rights. In the execution of these terms, the Supreme Commander ordered the annulment of all wartime legislations restricting the freedom of speech, press and thought, and as a result, political parties once more came into existence.

The Liberal Party, Progressive Party and Socialist Party (Social Democratic Party) came into being. The first two parties were not essentially different from the prewar " Seiyu-kai " and " Minsei-to " respectively, but the re-establishment of the Socialist Party was symbolic of the dawn of a new era in Japan.

The ban against the Communists was removed; their leaders were released from prison and the Japan Communist Party came into being anew.

The character of the various political parties is indicated by their respective attitudes toward the postwar Constitution of Japan.

The Liberal Party endeavored to keep intact the basic principles set forth in the Meiji Constitution establishing sovereignty in the

Emperor and recognizing the Imperial lineage through the centuries. However, it called for the abolition of such institutions as the emergency ordinance, independent ordinance, independent authority of the army and navy, proclamation of a state of siege and emergency Imperial prerogatives, in order to decrease the powers of the Government and decrease the powers of the Diet. It also advocated a bicameral Diet with the House of Representatives to be given precedence. The Liberal Party further desired that the State Ministers should be responsible to the Diet, and that the Prime Minister, as head of the cabinet, should stand above all the other State Ministers. It wanted the court of administrative litigation to be abolished and its authority transferred to ordinary courts of law. It believed that the scope of matters to be subject to administrative litigation should be enlarged and that the position of the Supreme Court should be enhanced. In a word, the Liberal Party was intent on strengthening the position of the Diet by adhering to the fundamental principles of the Meiji Constitution.

The Progressive Party took the same stand as the Liberal Party in regard to the maintenance of the Emperor system. It held the view that the Emperor should reign with the assistance of his subjects in conformity with the provisions of the Constitution. It agreed generally with the Liberal Party that the powers of the Diet should be strengthened by eliminating the independent command of the army and navy and the emergency Imperial prerogatives, that in a bicameral Diet the House of Representatives should be given priority, that the State Ministers should be responsible to the Diet and that the court of administrative litigation should be abolished. The Progressive Party differed from the Liberal Party on only one major point, that is, recognition of the importance of vesting in the Supreme Court the power to adjudge the validity of laws and orders.

Thus, both the Liberal and Progressive parties sought to avoid changes in the fundamental principles of the Meiji Constitution and made a special effort to preserve the Emperor system in its original form. During the period leading to the drafting of the new Constitution, there was a heated controversy on whether the Emperor system could be maintained in a democracy.

The Progressive Party explained its position on the issue in February 1946, as follows:

"Though some contend that monarchism is incompatible with democracy, government based on the people's will to support a monarchy could be called democratic government; such is the real end of constitutional monarchy...... We cannot endorse the theory that the Emperor shall be an organ of the State, or the view that although the Emperor system may be maintained, sovereign power shall reside with the people except such as may be retained in his hands; or the logic that unless the Emperor system is abolished by making him a mere ceremonial symbol, complete realization of democracy is impossible...... If the Emperor system were denied at this juncture and in its stead a republican form of government were adopted, the State would surely begin to crumble. We are firmly determined to reject all such views and arguments."

This opinion favoring the preservation of the Emperor system was fully supported by the Liberal Party.

On the other hand, the Socialist Party called for the establishment of a democratic government and resolute execution of a socialist economy as its fundamental policy and declared that its objectives were quite different from those of the Liberal and Progressive parties. It said it would recognize the Emperor system for the time being but emphasized that sovereign power should reside with the State (a national cooperative body which included the Emperor). It asserted that sovereign power should be divided between the Diet and the Emperor with the former taking the major part and the latter the remainder (with large-scale restrictions on Imperial prerogatives). The Socialists thus agreed to the preservation of the Emperor system. However. what they consented to was a system much nearer to that under the provisions of the new Constitution of Japan than that under the Meiji Constitution. The Socialists also wanted the Diet to be bicameral, with the House of Representatives to be given the superior position, that the second chamber be composed of members elected by vocational organizations, that the Cabinet be responsible to the Diet and that the court of administrative litigation be abolished. On these points the Socialist Party generally agreed with the Liberal and Progressive parties. But it went further by advocating the adoption of a recall system, the recognition of the right of all people to a decent living and establishment of the basic principles for a social State, points never before advocated by a political party in Japan.

While these three parties were generally agreed on the maintenance of the Emperor system, the Communist Party wholly opposed it and declared that Japan should be a people's republic in which sovereign power belonged to the people.

The respective attitudes of the four major postwar political parties toward the new Constitution were outlined above to indicate the general political trends in Japan after the war. The new Constitution was established quite independently of the will of these political parties—this matter will be referred to later in this chapter—and their views did not influence its drafting for all practical purposes. For example, both the Liberal and Progressive parties strongly advocated the preservation of the Emperor system on the basis of the Meiji Constitution but did not raise any objection to General MacArthur's draft of Japan's Constitution, which called for a radical change in the system. In the Diet all political parties bowed to the unavoidable trend of the times and unanimously voted approval of the MacArthur draft Constitution.

IV

Following Japan's surrender, widespread discussions were held in Japan regarding what should be done with the Meiji Constitution. Some argued that it should immediately be revised, while others contended that there was no need for alteration. The controversy came to an end when in October 1945, General MacArthur issued a directive to the Japanese Government, ordering it to prepare a revision of the Constitution. In response the Japanese Government, which was then under the leadership of Prime Minister Kijuro Shidehara, appointed a Committee for the Study of the Constitutional Problem and work was begun immediately.

State Minister Joji Matsumoto, chairman of the Committee, himself wrote a draft revision of the Constitution on the basis of the discussions of his committee, but as this draft has never been published its contents are not exactly known. However, it is believed that the draft on the whole included the views held by the Liberal and Progressive parties. Speaking in the Diet, Dr. Matsumoto said he desired to retain the fundamental principles of the Meiji Constitution, which declared the Emperor as the head of the State and as the holder of sovereign power.

The Matsumoto draft was completed in January 1946, and submitted to the Cabinet for study, but it was never acted on.

The Supreme Commander for the Allied Powers had been closely observing with deep concern the Japanese Government's work on the Constitutional problem and was greatly disappointed in the contents of the Matsumoto draft. He believed that such a Constitution as that drafted by Dr. Matsumoto could never result in the democratization of the government system of Japan and despaired of obtaining a truly democratic Constitution drafted by the Japanese Government.

General MacArthur, therefore, decided to draft a Constitution for Japan as a model to be given to the Japanese Government. Early in February 1946, he ordered his staff to write a draft Constitution for presentation to the Japanese Government. In about a week the draft was completed and submitted to General MacArthur. On February 13, 1946, Major-General Whitney, who was Chief of SCAP's Government Section, met Foreign Minister Shigeru Yoshida and State Minister Matsumoto, as representatives of the Japanese Government, and delivered to them the draft Constitution. He told them that the Supreme Commander for the Allied Powers wanted the Japanese Government to enact a Constitution modelled after his draft.

This action greatly surprised the Japanese Government, and Prime Minister Shidehara and other Ministers were dissatisfied with the MacArthur draft. They intended to make radical changes in the draft until they learned that the Supreme Commander was determined not to allow such changes.

Opposition of the Japanese Government to the MacArthur draft was quite natural. The Liberals and Progressives, as previously explained, were agreed in supporting the Emperor system based on the provisions of the Meiji Constitution, and even the Socialists did not go to the length of rejecting this system. In other words, the preservation of the Emperor system was favored by public opinion at that time in Japan. The MacArthur draft, on the other hand, withheld sovereign power from the Emperor and revolutionized the Emperor system by placing sovereignty in the hands of the people.

Japan, however, was not an independent State, and the Japanese Government and the people were subject to the authority of the Supreme Commander in the government of the country. Under such circumstances, with the Supreme Commander strongly desiring the adoption of his draft of the Japanese Constitution, the Japanese Government was in no position to ignore it regardless of the opinions of the people. As a consequence the Shidehara Cabinet adopted the MacArthur draft almost in its entirety and published it on March 6, 1946 as its own draft of the new Constitution. In other words, the Government which had been deliberating upon the Matsumoto draft announced as its own the MacArthur draft which was fundamentally different from the former.

The political parties then unanimously approved the so-called Government-draft Constitution. In light of the view expressed by these political parties regarding the revision of the Constitution, it would appear incomprehensible why they approved the " Government draft " so readily, but the situation becomes clear when it is realized that the draft was one submitted by General MacArthur as the Supreme Commander for the Allied Powers.

On April 10, 1946, one month after the publication of the Mac-Arthur draft as the Constitution proposed by the Shidehara Cabinet, a general election for the House of Representatives was held.

The election was most significant. Firstly, at the end of the preceding year the Diet, under a directive from General MacArthur, passed a law conferring on men and wowen alike the right to vote and the right to hold public office. Thus, Japanese women obtained those rights which had formerly been given only to the men. The April 1946 election was the first in Japanese history in which women voted. April 10 has since been observed annually as "Women's Day" in commemoration of this epochal event.

Secondly, candidates for election to the House of Representatives were given the opportunity to reveal their personal views on the draft Constitution while the people on their part were enabled to indicate their attitude towards it by their votes. But it would be a mistake to place too much importance on this aspect of the problem. At this time the press was under control, legally and actually, in line with the occupation policy of the Allied Powers, and criticisms of the draft Constitution were not made in wholly free circumstances. Tha fact that the MacArthur draft of the Constitution was published over a month before the general election does not mean that the Japanese people had had been given ample time and opportunity to discuss it on its merits.

The draft Constitution was submitted to the Diet in accordance with Article 23 of the Meiji Constitution, and the House of Peers and the House of Representatives both passed it with a majority of over two-thirds of the members. On obtaining the sanction of the Emperor, Japan's new Constitution was promulgated on November 3, 1946 and came into force on May 3, 1947.

V

The new Constitution of Japan was based fully on the principles of democracy. It lay special emphasis on the fundamental human rights. The freedom of political speech, press and association was guaranteed. The fact must nevertheless be pointed out here that Japan was not then an independent State, and she did not achieve independence until the Japanese Peace Treaty came into force in April 1952.

While the new Constitution guaranteed the fundamental human rights and the freedom of speech, press and assembly, the sovereignty of Japan was limited by the authority of the Supreme Commander. No action of the Supreme Commander could be restrained by the Japanese Constitution, and his acts were therefore often called "super-constitutional" and his will, "categorically imperative."

It was under such conditions that Japan was governed during the Allied Occupation. Real freedom of speech, press and assembly was reserved for the future, until Japan recovered full independence.

Japan became an independent country in April 1952, and her Constitution then became completely effective. The time then arrived for the political parties to begin full activity by making complete use of the guaranteed freedom of speech, press and association.

The Liberal and other political parties which had been established following the war's end were unable during the Occupation to be thoroughly consistent with respective ideals. Today they can.

How they will appeal to the people to obtain public support for those ideals and thereby contribute toward the realization of a parliamentary cabinet and party government provided for by the new Constitution of Japan remains to be seen.

DEMOCRATIZATION OF JAPANESE ADMINISTRATION OF JUSTICE

By Dr. Kotaro Tanaka

Chief Justice of the Supreme Court of Japan

Since the Meiji Restoration of 1868, the judicial system of Japan has been patterned after European systems—first the French, then the German. The Prussian Constitution influenced the Meiji Constitution of 1889, which divided state power among the legislative, executive and judicial branches of government under a constitutional monarchy, following Montesquieu's principle of the separation of the three powers. Under this Constitution judicial power was exercised by the court in the name of the Emperor, with whom sovereign authority resided. The position of judges was guaranteed, and seldom, if ever, did the executive interfere with a judgment of the court. The administration of the courts, however, came under the Ministry of Justice and the Justice Minister was a member of the Cabinet. From the standpoint of system, the courts were, therefore, subordinate to the executive and the independence of judges was no more than relative.

In the case of legislation, both substantive and procedural, the Continental principles of law-making were adopted; instead of the common law or case law principle of Anglo-Saxon nations, the codification principle of Continental jurisprudence was followed. The Civil Code, Commercial Code, Criminal Code, Code of Civil Procedure and Code of Criminal Procedure were successively enacted. In compiling the Civil Code some consideration was given to a few ancient customs in the Law of Family Relations and Law of Succession, but in the main German law, which stemmed from Roman law, was regarded as the mother law. The other laws mentioned also generally followed German patterns, except that in the Company Law of the

Commercial Code some elements of Anglo-American law were introduced in recent years.

It must also be pointed out that trends of jurisprudence and law
education in the universities were generally styled after German
models. Losing sight of the aim of laws and regulations, scholars
often devoted themselves exclusively to the study of theoretical or
interpretive jurisprudence which was out of touch with the other
social sciences and the demands of society. They crammed their
minds full of systematized, abstract theories which were by no means
suitable for developing legal minds and reasoning ability. Such
tendencies, coupled with an educational method based exclusively on
lectures, hindered the development of jurisprudence and the improvement of the legal profession. Legal procedure, which should be a
practical matter, was made complicated because of systems of procedural law which had had a theoretical and unnatural development.
Consequently, attorneys, forgetting the original aim of a lawsuit,
often would play a game of legal cat and mouse among themselves
or devote their energies to trying to trip up the court over a legal
technicality. The slow settlement of lawsuits has thus become a
chronic disease of legal life.

The new democratic and pacifist Constitution of Japan has served
to bring about many radical reforms in all branches of national administration. The reform of the judicial system was one of the most
important achievements. This reform would never have been effected
had it not been strongly backed by the Occupation, and the same
can be said about reform in other branches of the administration.
However, in the case of judicial reform, it is especially noteworthy
that there was always comparatively close cooperation between the
the Occupation authorities and the Japanese government and judicial
circles. The principal reason for this was that the judicial reforms
did not necessitate any compromise or accommodation of conflicting
interests, all discussions centering on such technical considerations
as might be required to attain the goal of the reform.

Under the new Constitution, judicial power is vested in a Supreme

Court and in such inferior courts as are established by law (Article 76, Paragraph 1). This hierarchal organization of ordinary courts shall have all judicial power, and such extraordinary tribunals as the Administrative Court and a Court Martial—which, needless to say, presupposes existence of armed forces—shall not be established (Article 76, Paragraph 2). The defunct Administrative Court had jurisdiction over a very limited number of matters; at present a suit against any illegal act of an executive agency is to be brought to an ordinary court of law. In cases where an executive agency has competency to receive an appeal of findings, proceedings of the court of the first instance shall be taken in the executive agency and the law-court shall function as a tribunal of not lower than the second instance. In brief, the courts under the new system have jurisdiction not only in civil and criminal cases as they had in the past, but also in administrative litigation in a broad sense (such as cases pertaining to taxes, labor, agricultural land, education and self-government). All lawsuits concerning elections come under the jurisdiction of law-courts at present, as in the past.

The most important power given the court by the new Constitution is the authority to examine the constitutionality of any law, order or official act. This corresponds to the power of judicial review, known in the United States as the system of "checks and balances" of the judicial branch over the legislative and executive. This power was established in the United States by Chief Justice John Marshall (1755–1835) of the Supreme Court during his 34-year tenure of office, and it is still maintained. But it is a right not yet recognized by the legal organization of any country on the Continent. Japan, which had followed the Continental legal system, did not recognize it until the revision of the Constitution.

The power of review is based on Article 81 of the Constitution, which states: "The Supreme Court is the court of last resort with power to determine the constitutionality of any law, order, regulation or official act." In reality, interpretations of this provision are not entirely free from doubt. Some jurists are of the opinion that even in cases where a suit was not brought on any concrete question, the Supreme Court has the power to pronounce its abstract decision on the constitutionality of given legislation as the court of first instance and last resort. Mr. Mosaburo Suzuki, chairman of the Central Executive Committee of the Left Wing Socialist Party, brought in 1952 a suit directly to the Supreme Court, petitioning for the nullification of the law and orders establishing the National Police Reserve. On October 8, 1952 the Supreme Court dismissed Suzuki's claim on the grounds that under the present system it had no power to give an abstract judgment on the case.

During the past five years under the new court system, the Supreme Court has not yet used its power of review to label any law or order unconstitutional. However, the fact that the Supreme Court is now the court of last resort with the power to determine the constitutionality of any law shows a remarkable elevation of its position compared to the courts under the old system. Above all, this system completes the protection of fundamental human rights guaranteed to the people by the new Constitution.

Of course, the old Constitution also guaranteed various rights and freedoms, but these were subject to restriction by legislation of the Diet. Under the new Constitution oppressive legislation is impossible because any law restricting human rights and freedoms will become invalid. It is the Supreme Court's duty to protect these fundamental human rights and freedoms by nullifying restrictive legislation through judgment of a test case. This is why the Supreme Court is popularly called the "Keeper of the Constitution."

In the eyes of the new Constitution, the fundamental human rights and freedoms were not created by the State. They are eternal and universal, common to all men, antecede the State and are founded upon natural law. (See the Preamble and Article 11.) But the people shall refrain from any abuse of these rights and freedoms, and shall always be responsible for utilizing them for the public welfare (Article 12). Public welfare is derived from the natural character of a body politic called the State. It is the duty of the

Supreme Court to determine the limitations placed on these two concepts by investigations of actual cases before the court.

In order to enable the Supreme Court and the inferior courts to discharge their duties in a satisfactory manner, their independence must be guaranteed. There are two facets to such independence—one for the judges and one for the courts. Although the independence of judges was virtually provided for by the old Constitution, the new Constitution made it more complete. Judges' salaries, which formerly were below those of officials in the executive branch, are now a little higher than in the executive. Of the judges of the Supreme Court, the Chief Justice is to be appointed directly by the Emperor under the provisions in the Constitution, as is also true of the Prime Minister (Article 6, Paragraph 2). The fourteen other judges of the high court are accorded the same status as that of Ministers of State. The Chief Justice receives the same remuneration as the Prime Minister, while all the other judges are given the same salary as the Ministers of State. The Cabinet has the power to determine the appointment of the Chief Justice and the other judges. Here it should be noted that the appointment of each judge is to be reviewed by the people every ten years. This corresponds to endorsement by the Senate of the United States and is in substance an instrument of recall (Article 79). The judges of the Supreme Court and the inferior courts are all appointed. The age of 70 years is set as the mandatory retirement age of judges of the Supreme Court and of the summary courts, the latter corresponding to justices of the peace. Retirement is required at 65 for judges of the other courts.

The judges of the Supreme Court are not exclusively career judges, in contrast to the make-up of the "Dai Shin In" (Supreme Court) of the old system, which closely resembled the Court of Cassation in Europe. About one-third of the new Supreme Court is made up of career judges. The rest are men who have distinguished themselves as attorneys, practitioners of Constitutional or Administrative Law, professors of law or diplomats. The formation of the Supreme Court by specialists in Criminal and Civil Law as well as men of varied knowledge and experience is due largely to the expansion of the powers of the court which now has the power of review already mentioned. In other words, it is the answer to the demand for far-sighted, high level judgment, which might be called statesmanship.

In the general selection of judges, present-day Japan has a long way to go to reach the level of uniformity in jurisprudence found in the United States where judges are chosen from the common pools of the Bar Associations. In order to become a judge, public procurator or attorney, a student who has graduated from a university and passed the State Judiciary Examination is required to study legal practice for two years at a special training school such as the Judicial Institute for Training and Research under the jurisdiction of the Supreme Court.

There are now approximately 6,000 attorneys-at-law in Japan. They have organized and maintain law associations by area and have a national federation of law associations. The Attorneys Law of 1949, which governs affairs of attorneys and law associations, released attorneys from the supervision of the State and gave the law associations almost complete freedom. This will certainly serve to advance the social standing of attorneys, which was not very high in the past. It should be noted that until recently Japan did not have any organizations like the bar associations of the United States which are very influential not only in the judicial world but in social circles as well. U.S. bar associations are made up not only of attorneys, but also of judges, state's attorneys, law professors and other jurists.

Such an organization is very important for Japan because it is absolutely necessary to ensure coordination of the independent activities of various judicial circles in order to attain the goals of our judiciary. This is why a Bar Association was established in 1952 after a few years of preparations. Whether or not the new Bar Association will mature soundly, discharge its mission to cooperate with the courts and become as potent a social force as its sister institutions in the United States remains to be seen.

In the area of independence of the courts, the new system is bolstered by the provision for the Supreme Court to carry on the administration of the internal affairs of the courts through a conference body of its 15 judges. At present they meet once a week to determine the institution, revision or annulment of rules; the appointment of judges of lower courts and other personnel affairs, and court budgets and other court business. In this way, the administration of the courts—formerly under the jurisdiction of the Ministry of Justice—has been completely separated from politics. The Attorney General who is a Cabinet member is authorized to handle affairs pertaining to the public procurator's office, the registration and execution of penalties being his major concern. The Attorney General's original title of "Homu Sosai" has recently been changed to "Homu Daijin" (Minister of Justice) and the scope of his authority has been somewhat modified.

In that the Chief Justice of the Supreme Court is not a member of the Cabinet, his position differs from that of the Lord Chancellor of England. It also differs from that of the Chief Justice of the U.S. Supreme Court because the Japanese Chief Justice heads the administration of court affairs. Besides being the first judge of the land, he presides over the conference of judges that oversees the various administrative affairs.

As a consequence of the Supreme Court being in charge of court adminstration, a Secretariat comparable in size to that of the former Ministry of Justice has been established.

The Supreme Court's most important power is its power to make rules. The Court is vested with the power to make rules governing procedures, matters concerning attorneys, internal discipline of the courts and administration of judicial affairs (Article 77, Paragraph 1). About 150 rules have been laid down by the Supreme Court since its establishment in the summer of 1947. These rules provide for procedure of civil and criminal cases, organization of the courts and particulars of judicial administration. The judges of the present Court disagree on the scope of the court's rule-making powers. Some of them argue that since the law is superior to rules, the latter can be instituted only within the scope of the former. Others contend that the law can be modified by a rule, while still others insist that the law and the rules stand on an equal footing so that in cases where they conflict, the issue can be settled by determining which has precedence according to its date of enforcement. For the present, the Supreme Court has been setting rules for regulation of details within the scope of the law.

As already mentioned, the courts and the judges enjoy a remarkably higher position than they did under the old system. Judicial power has gained complete independence as the third division of state power, on the same level as the executive and the legislative. If there developed any encroachment on the powers of the judiciary by the legislative, executive or any other organ, the very foundations of democracy would be endangered because the judiciary aims at maintenance of legal order based on guarantees of freedom and justice.

A few years ago a controversy arose between the legislative branch and the Court over the provisions of Article 62 of the Constitution which gives the two houses of the Diet the power to investigate matters in the government. The controversy was over whether or not this included the power to investigate the courts. Under the same article, each house of the Diet is also empowered to subpoena witnesses and records for their investigations. In this case, the Judiciary Committee of the House of Councillors had started investigations and criticized the penalties fixed and other matters of a judgment of an inferior court which had come under fire by the public. The Judiciary Committee had acted before final judgment had been established. A meeting of judges of the Supreme Court then issued an open letter, in the name of the proxy of the Chief Justice, addressed to the President of the House of Councillors dated May 20, 1949. This protested that the acts of the Committee overstepped its power and that the power to inquire into the justice of a judgment or to investigate facts and penalties in a case belongs exclusively to the courts which are invested with judicial powers and that the Diet cannot use such powers on the strength of Article 62 of the Constitution. Moreover, there are not infrequent cases where a party dissatisfied with the judgment of a court has petitioned the Judges Prosecution Committee for action under the Judge Impeachment Law. All this is due to a misunderstanding of the spirit of the impeachment system. Fortunately, there so far has been no case in which the Judge Prosecution Committee has accepted such a petition and demanded the dismissal of a judge by impeachment.

The courts and the judges have indeed been entrusted with very important powers under the new Constitution, but have they really acquired a social position corresponding to their responsibility? If measured by the standards of England and the United States, we regret to confess that in Japan recognition of the important position of the courts and respect for judges by the people are still very low. This can be surmised from the tone of public opinion reflected in the newspapers regarding the review by the people of five judges of the Supreme Court. This took place at the same time as the 1952 general election for the House of Representatives. It is very doubtful that the majority of the people who cast ballots that day were familiar either with the decisions made by the five judges and their written opinions, or their characters, wisdom or personal histories. The people are too preoccupied wlth the problems of everyday living—fluctuating prices, food rationing, taxes, admission of children to school, commuting, etc.—to pay much attention to the fact that the maintenance of social order by means of the justice of the courts is the cornerstone of a democratic community. Consequently, the people showed little interest in the review of the judges and votes for dismissal of each candidate averaged about 10 per cent of the total ballots. It is possible that those dismissal votes were cast chiefly on instructions from leaders of trade unions to their members or by agitation of the Communist Party and some elements of other left-wing parties. This review system is now the target of a great deal of criticism on its significance and operation, and an amendment is being urged. It is an undeniable fact, however, that the system has been instrumental in impressing the importance of the Supreme Court on the minds of the people.

Maintenance of order in the courts and expediting decisions of cases are the two most important problems now confronting the courts of Japan.

Before the end of World War II, the judicial annals of Japan record almost no case where the order of the court was disturbed during a public trial. After the end of the war, political freedoms—freedoms of speech, press and assembly—were given to the people and the leaders of the Japanese Communist Party who were serving jail sentences were promptly released. Since then the Communist Party, in collusion with Communist-dominated countries, has become increasingly active in politics, economics, labor, etc. Their activities have become aberrant, subversive and exceedingly damaging to the order of State and community, and many have been in violation of criminal law. It is natural that under these conditions the Communists and their sympathizers should have begun to scheme to turn the courtroom into a stage for their struggles and propaganda. Provisions of the Code of Criminal Procedure, the customary way of enforcing it and the mentality of the judges have been unable effectively to control defendants and attorneys of a particular kind and spectators who would not hesitate to do everything conceivable to encourage such defendants and attorneys by capitalizing on the principle of public trial. Furthermore, Japanese judges have no system of " contempt of court " to which they can resort. Certainly, the Criminal Code provides punishment for acts that would obstruct performance of public duties or interfere with a trial in court. But even these provisions are not being used in practice to control threats, abuse, uproar and other obstructive acts at a trial, out of consideration to the preservation of evidence and the convenience of prosecution. A law to maintain order in court, patterned after the British and American system, was enacted last summer, but it is impossible to tell how effective it will be in certain types of cases, especially mass trials. It is doubtful that a 20-day detention and a ¥30,000 fine as maximum penalty—though these are not criminal penalties—can ever control the Communists who, denying the Constitution, the power of the State and the authority of the courts, are doing everything conceivable to defy them. It is also not certain that the new law will be able to ensure the inviolability of the court and the smooth progress of trials. In any case, it is most desirable that judges endeavor to sit in judgment of cases of this kind and hand down just decisions, while maintaining high moral courage and the dignity of the court.

The slow progress of litigation has been a world-wide evil since ancient times. In Japan it has become a chronic disease. Anyone with a little common sense knows that in Japan minor civil cases—for example, the disputes that occur almost daily over rented houses or lots—would take at least three years to reach final judgment, were they to go to the court of last resort. Nor would a criminal case be decided quickly, in case an appeal to higher courts is made. In October 1952 a judgment of a court of first instance was given in a bribery case which involved some well-known politicians and many businessmen. Counting from the date of indictment, these defendants awaited the decision of the court for periods ranging from four years and four days to three years and 10 months. If they should appeal, and the trial in the higher courts proceeds at the same rate of speed, how many years more would elapse before the case receives the final judgment of the court? This delay on the bribery case is being bitterly criticized by the press. If such conditions continue, realization of justice and protection of fundamental human rights by the court will be almost impossible. Furthermore, the continued trust of the people in the courts could not be expected.

In order to improve the situation, judges must rid themselves of the inefficient, easy-going ways of bygone days in their handling of cases. Justice as a rule calls for several qualities—the correct interpretation of law, using scholarship; the pursuit of truth, using the methods of a historian, and efficiency in practice. In this country, judges have been used to giving conscientious attention to the first and second qualities, but often did not pay much attention to the third. The juridical conscience should be aroused so that equal and careful attention is given to cultivating all three qualities. The Japanese judges ought always to keep in mind the maxim: "Justice delayed, justice denied."

Prompt justice, however, will never be realized by proper mental preparation and the efforts of the judges alone. Attorneys share the responsibility with the courts for slow justice in Japan. Simply out of a desire to have smooth proceedings, a judge usually assents to the petition of an attorney who, not being prepared by a set date, pleads postponement of a hearing more than once or petitions for examination of useless evidence. Again, an individual who may have lost a civil case in a lower court, or his attorney, will often appeal to a higher court—even though fully aware of the hopelessness of the case—with the sole purpose of delaying as long as possible the execution of the judgment. In criminal cases, too, a guilty defendant or his counsel will often appeal to a higher court to delay the execution of his sentence.

Both the Civil and the Criminal Codes have some provisions designed to prevent abuse of the right to appeal, but these provisions are seldom applied to an actual case. Moreover, Article 31 of the Constitution states that criminal penalties shall not be imposed, except by due process of the law. Consequently, attorneys would not fail to use the slightest trespass or deviation of procedure in a lower court—even though it would have no bearing on the outcome of the trial—as a pretext to appeal to a higher court on the basis of a violation of the Constitution. Because of these circumstances, the Supreme Court has currently as many as 7,000 cases pending, and is kept busy disposing of them. It is necessary for the judges to keep in mind that time is not their property or that of any individual, but is a public treasure. It is also necessary that attorneys cooperate in speeding up the proceedings.

In summation, a new system for democratization of the Japanese judicial system has been established by the new Constitution. In order to make it function as a part of our society instead of keeping it as a mere paper plan, the people must have a deeper understanding of the judicial system, and judicial officials will have to exert greater efforts. Although the system has been transformed, its substance is still not entirely free from traditions or old habits and customs. The judges, public procurators and attorneys must realize that they are not opponents but partners working for the realization of the common goal of maintaining law and order and ensuring justice and the protection of freedom.

One may ask, then, how can we solidify such belief and destroy the evils present in our judicial system, so that the system may satisfy all reasonable demands of the people? By way of an answer, I should like to request the judicial branch to take a universal point of view on two things. In Japan, the actual business of judicial proceedings has been somewhat neglected in favor of jurisprudence. Therefore, the first thing we must do is to be critical from an international standpoint and examine the things we are actually doing. Fortunately such an atmosphere is gradually being created in this country. Trips of jurists to and from Japan have been frequent since the end of the war, and quite a number of Japanese judges, public procurators and attorneys have visited the United States. While there they studied the operation of the judicial system and the legal profession, and on returning to Japan they have offered suggestions which have stimulated moves to improve our judicial administration. Recently these useful inspection trips by jurists have been made not only to the United States, but also to England and other countries. It is certain that the presence of Japanese delegates or observers at the international conferences of jurists held in Berlin and Madrid last summer helped the Japanese jurists to recognize the universal nature of the mission of justice and to feel keenly the necessity of cooperation of all nations for the realization of their common objectives.

Secondly, such cooperation of various nations understanding the universal objects of justice will be possible only when they acknowledge the universal existence of a basic rule for justice and freedom for all mankind. This basic rule is nothing more than Natural Law. These are the ethical principles on which are based the Charter of the United Nations, the Declaration of Universal Human Rights of 1948 and our own Constitution. The recognition and the negation of those principles characterizes the existence on the globe of two opposing groups: the free nations and the nations behind the Iron Curtain. The confrontation of these two worlds has its origin in the difference in their attitudes toward acknowledging the fundamental principles of Natural Law, which is based on efforts to achieve humanism in the true sense. Mutual cooperation of all free nations in efforts to protect and realize Natural Law is an indispensable condition for democratizing the whole world, securing lasting peace and guarding the welfare of humanity. The judicial branches of all nations are shouldering such universal duties in their own areas. The mission of the Japanese judicial branch, too, is to do its own share in this universal mission.

AN APPRAISAL OF EDUCATIONAL REFORMS IN JAPAN

By Daishiro Hidaka

Former Vice Minister of Education

EDUCATIONAL REFORM IN JAPAN

Education in Japan has undergone a striking metamorphosis since the end of World War II in August 1945. Basic concepts, administration, organization, curricula and teaching methods have been thoroughly revamped to conform with Japan's new role in the society of nations.

Here is the story of what has been done and how it was done. Here also is a picture of education in Japan today, and an outline of the problems that must be met in the future.

1. First Steps in the Reform

Emergency Measures

The ground-breaking for democratization of the Japanese educational system was initiated by the Japanese Government in compliance with a series of memoranda and directives issued by the Supreme Commander for the Allied Powers (SCAP).

In October 1945 the spread of militaristic and ultra-nationalistic ideologies was prohibited. In order to carry out this directive, teachers were carefully screened, and those that were found to be unfit for their jobs were dismissed. In December of the same year measures were taken (a) to prevent the guiding spirit of and faith in Shintoism from being utilized as a medium for the spread of nationalistic or super-patriotic ideologies and (b) to prohibit the teaching of ethical training, Japanese history and geography because the courses of study and text books were strongly prejudiced in the direction of ultra-nationalism.

These first emergency measures were taken to purge the field of education of feudalistic and militaristic elements.

Rebuilding for democracy

A United States Education Mission arrived in Tokyo in March 1946. The 27-member mission toured Japan for a month. After studying Japanese conditions, seeking the views of many Japanese educators on educational problems and mapping out a program, they submitted their report to General Douglas MacArthur, the Supreme Allied Commander. That report contained an overall plan for reform and democratization of Japanese education "from the standpoint of the experienced educators who believe in the innumerable potential powers of the human being in seeking freedom and individual and social development."

The report was well received by the Japanese and was considered to have been drawn up with skill and fair-mindedness. It is now generally appreciated as having had a tremendous direct and indirect effect on subsequent educational reforms enacted in Japan.

Upon completion of the education report the Japanese committee which had cooperated with the U.S. Education Mission to Japan was dissolved and the Education Reform Committee was established in August 1946. (The name of the committee was changed to the Japan Education Reforms Commission in June 1949.) This group of about fifty persons, most of them leading scholars and educators with years of practical experience, performed yeoman service before it ended its mission in June 1951. It established nineteen Special Sub-Committees, studied in detail various educational questions and submitted thirty-four concrete reform programs to the Prime Minister.

The Ministry of Education, acting on the recommendations of the committee, prepared bills and submitted them to the Diet with the approval of SCAP. These eventually were enacted into new education laws. The committee was actually responsible for the basic concept of educational reforms put into practice in postwar Japan. The Ministry of Education, for its part, deserves credit for drawing up bills based on the committee recommendations and enforcing the laws after they had been enacted.

Prewar educational policies were drafted by the Ministry of Education and were arbitrarily thrust upon educational institutions in the form of Imperial or Departmental ordinances. This form of administrative ordinance has now been abolished. The Ministry of Education, prepares bills for the Diet upon the recommendation of such democratic advisory organs as the Education Reforms Commission and the Council for the Establishment of Universities. There are now more than ten such laws to govern educational affairs enacted since the end of the war.

II. Changes in Educational Principles—Basis for Democracy

The Fundamental Law of Education, one of the new laws enacted after the war, might be called the "constitution of education" in new-born Japan. The preamble states that "the law has been enacted for purpose of clarifying the objects of education and also to establish the basis for the education of a new Japan in line with the spirit of the Japanese Constitution." The fundamental principles underlying the law are progressive liberalism and humanistic democracy looking toward freedom and peace. The law provides that:

1. The objectives of education are to bring up the individuals of a nation in order to consummate their personalities, to foster love of truth and justice as the components of a peaceful nation and to imbue society with a spirit of independence.

2. In order to realize the above objectives, it shall be a principle of education to allow freedom of study, cultivate a spirit of spontaneity, encourage the individual to exert himself toward contributing to the creation and development of culture and to learn to pay due respect to and cooperate with others.

3. Equal opportunity of education shall be given to every member of the nation in accordance with his ability.

4. Every child of school age shall complete nine years of compulsory education.

5. There shall be co-education of boys and girls without discrimination and on the basis of mutual understanding and cooperation among them.

6. Schools are established for the benefit of the nation as a whole, and teachers shall perform their duties and obligations to meet the purpose. Fair treatment to teachers shall be guaranteed accordingly.

7. Social education shall be given assistance and encouragement.

8. Proper understanding of political affairs shall be fostered among the students, but education on political affairs shall be free from partisan political thought in any public schools.

9. Religious tolerance and the importance of religion in life shall be taught, but public schools shall not promote any specific religion.

10. Educational administration shall be carried out under the principle of local autonomy and to serve the nation as a whole.

The Fundamental Law of Education has thus become the charter of Japan's postwar education, replacing the Imperial Rescript on Education which had heretofore been the sole basic educational doctrine. The Imperial Rescript on Education was the fundamental national moral code given to the nation by the Emperor Meiji in 1890. It played a very important role in creating a unified, modern Japan, and helped to break down the ancient feudal system. It contained teachings of high moral standards applicable not only to Japan but to all nations, but it over-emphasized the semi-feudalistic idea of complete obedience and loyalty to the Imperial Family. Because some ideas expressed in the Rescript were not consistent with the spirit of the new Constitution, it was nullified by the Diet in June 1948.

III. Evolving Education Reforms—Equal Opportunities for All

In keeping with the fundamental revision of educational doctrine, a great change has taken place in postwar educational system.

Compulsory education was established in Japan in 1872. The original system was based on the French system. It underwent repeated reforms, but the recent ones are the most sweeping ever undertaken. The prewar school system was based on six years of compulsory standard primary school. There were three types of courses within the system:

1) Six years of primary school on compulsory basis; five years of secondary education; three years of high school and three years of university education. (Medical schools maintained a four-year course.)

2) Six years of compulsory education in primary school; technical school of secondary school standards which specialized in agriculture, industry and commerce; technical college for higher technical training given to those graduated from secondary school, agricultural school, commercial school or industrial school.

3) Six years of compulsory primary school; a two-year supplementary course established for those who were unable to attend any secondary school. A special technical training course was also set up in the form of a Youths School for those who were forced to give up their schooling primarily because of economic reasons.

There were great differences in the three different programs in the quality of teachers, facilities, curricula, kind and standards of education. Consequently the social standing a person could achieve was often decided by the kind of school from which he had graduated. In general women received discriminatory treatment in the school system and were given few opportunities for higher education.

March of 1947 saw the School Education Law enacted in keeping with the spirit of the Fundamental Law of Education. It accomplished the unification of various educational systems then extant and also brought equal opportunity of education nearer reality.

The so-called 6-3-3-4 system has now come to be the only school system in postwar Japan. In the new school system the primary school course of six years is begun when children reach the age of six. This plus the three-year junior high school course constitutes the required nine years of compulsory education. Advanced education is given in the three-year senior high school course and the four-year university course. A kindergarten for tots from three to five years old is also included in the regular school system.

Primary School

The primary school system has not been changed except for the curriculum. The new curriculum includes the standard Japanese language, mathematics, social affairs, science, music, drawing, domestic science and physical education. The course in domestic science is given to children in the fifth and sixth grades for three hours each week.

Junior High School

The junior high school curriculum is divided into required and elective subjects. The required subjects are the standard Japanese language, social affairs, mathematics, science, music, drawing, health and physical education, vocational training and domestic science. The electives include such subjects as foreign languages, vocational training and domestic science. There is also a third category of subjects that include such special educational activities as sports, hobbies, amusements and other student activities. The privileges of universal education are also extended to the often-neglected handicapped children who may also receive nine years of training in schools for the blind, deaf, dumb and mentally retarded.

Senior High School

Senior high school subjects are classified as general or vocational. To be eligible for graduation the student must complete at least eighty-five units during the three-year course. One unit's credit is given for each fifty-minute class period in a thirty-five week school year.

Of the eighty-five units needed for graduation, thirty-eight units of general subjects are required and forty-seven units are elective. In the vocational courses, at least thirty units of agriculture, industry, commerce, fisheries, domestic science, handicrafts, etc. are needed in addition to the standard required subjects for graduation.

There is also a special high school and correspondence school system for working youths who are unable to attend regular high schools.

University

The universities are established to offer broad and rich cultural training to as many young people as possible, on the basis of equal educational opportunity for all. The program is designed to increase the number of potential leaders equipped with various skills and techniques and well-correlated knowledge.

The course of study in a university is based on four years of work under the unit system. One unit of credit is given for each three hours of lecture per week for a fifteen-week period. Each university sets its own curriculum on the basis of a "university standard" set by the University Establishment Council which will be dealt with later.

A total of 124 units is required for a bachelor's degree. These include at least thirty-six units of human, social and natural sciences; at least eighty-four units of required and elective subjects, and four units of physical education.

Pre-dental and pre-medical students are required to complete sixty units during the first two years of the regular four-year university course. They then enter four years of training in dental or medical schools. After they complete the four-year professional course they must serve a year of internship in a recognized hospital and pass a government examination before they are awarded a doctor's or dentist's license.

In order to broaden the benefits of university education, seminars and correspondence courses are being set up for those who are unable to attend regular university courses.

Junior College

The junior college system is comparatively new to Japan. It was established in June 1949 after the revision of the School Education

Law. The junior college offers two or three year courses of a semi-vocational and semi-specialized nature. The curriculum includes subjects related to natural and social science and the arts. Two units of physical education are required, incluing one unit of lecture. The curricula vary according to the specialty of the junior college, each college setting its particular course of study.

In two-year junior colleges sixty-two units are required for graduation. The requirement in a three-year junior college is ninety-three units. Units are calculated on the same basis as in the regular four-year universities. The curriculum in junior colleges is planned so that it will be convenient for students to advance to a four-year university in case they want to do so.

Post-Graduate Studies

Post-graduate courses at the universities are established to provide opportunities for advanced, detailed studies of theoretical and applied sciences and of the humanities.

For a master's degree a student must have his thesis accepted after he has completed a full year's study and at least thirty units in his specific field.

To satisfy the requirements for a doctor's degree the student must attend at least three years of classes, complete at least fifty units in his special field of study, submit a doctoral dissertation on original research and pass final examinations.

IV. Reform in Administration of Education

Three laws have wrought fundamental changes in educational administration—the Board of Education Law of July 1948; the Education Ministry Establishment Law of May 1949, and the Private Schools Law.

The guiding principles for the reform were laid out along three basic lines:

Democratization: Article 10 of the Fundamental Law of Education states that education shall be carried out in full recognition of its responsibility to the nation. This meant that bureaucratic and uniform control enforced by the government in the past had to be discarded. Instead the will of the people is to be carefully reflected in carrying out the administration of education. In other words, now any decisions on questions of education must be made by law enacted by the Diet representing the will of the people and not by administrative order of the government.

Decentralization: With the establishment of a system of boards of education this principle was carried out. One by one the powers that had theretofore been concentrated in the Education Ministry have been transferred to the local administrations. The Education Ministry's role has thus changed from one of a national administrative agency of compulsory education to one of giving advice to local boards of education on specific educational and technical questions. Self-rule has also been given to the universities under the administration of the Education Ministry.

Autonomy: Article 10 of the Fundamental Law of Education requires that education be guaranteed autonomy without any undue outside pressure. The function of educational administration is now to further various conditions necessary for the achievement of educational objectives and to serve the various educational activities. The Ministry no longer tries to hand down orders or exert influence over the activities of the various educational institutions. Educational administration is to be kept free from other administration in the country. Consequently, the boards of education are separated from the Education Ministry and also independent of the local autonomous bodies.

Boards of Education

Boards of education were set up in November of 1948 under the Board of Education Law enacted in July of that year. Ninety-seven boards of education were established in forty six prefectures, five major cities and forty six cities, towns and villages. In November 1952 the number increased by 10,000, adding boards that were established in cities, towns and villages all over the country.

The boards of education are a council-type administrative organ empowered to make decisions and implement policies pertaining to education, science and cultural affairs in the area under its jurisdiction. There are two principal kinds of boards—the prefectural boards and the city, town and village boards. The prefectural board of education has seven members; the city, town or village board has five. At least one member of each board is selected from the members of the Assembly of the local autonomous body; the others are selected by the people by means of direct election. The term of office is four years with half of the members being elected every two years.

The superintendent of education is a licensed specialist in educational administration who is under the control and supervision of the board. He handles all administrative affairs on education and also offers advice and recommendations to the board of education in his capacity as chief of the secretariat of the board.

The boards of education are empowered to supervise educational institutions below the level of senior high schools established by the local autonomous bodies. They may appoint or dismiss teachers and other personnel of the said institutions, prepare the education budget and submit it to the local Assembly through the chief of the autonomous body. The prefectural boards of education also are empowered to administer the issuance of teacher's licenses.

Supervision of Private Schools

Half of the schools in Japan are privately supported. These are governed under the Private School Law of December 1949 which became effective in March 1950.

Each private school is guided under its own principles and mode of education which are fully respected by the law. However, private schools come under the " public institutions " described in Article 6 of the Fundamental Law of Education and therefore the management of private schools comes within the scope of the law.

The Private School Law provides that the supervisory power of the government shall be exercised to the minimum in order to maintain the independence of the private schools. Before any decisions can be made pertaining to privately supported institutions, the Ministry of Education must first consult the Private University Council in case of universities or the Private School Council in case of private schools of senior high school level or below.

In order to ensure the " public nature " of private shools, regulations governing the establishment and operation of private schools provide that :

—The number of executives shall be fixed by law so as to check arbitrary action by minority members.

—Standards shall be established for the selection of executives.

—Measures shall be taken to assure that executive posts shall not be monopolized by the members of any one family.

—Councillors shall be appointed to advise the executives.

—The state and local autonomous bodies are authorized to give financial aid to private schools. The Private School Improvement Law was enacted in 1951, paving the way for private schools to accept financial aid from the state and local autonomous bodies.

Law for Supervision of National Universities

Even in the past, universities were given a high degree of autonomy, the professors council being the key policy organ. This body was often criticized as being self-complacent and dogmatic in its attitudes. In order to assure freedom of study and to maintain proper relationship between the university and society, the Education Ministry had been drafting a Law to eliminate undue control from inside the university and unreasonable interference from the outside.

Then in October 1948 the Civil Information and Education Section of SCAP approached the Japanese Government with a draft plan of a law that outlined the management of universities. The question of university administration reform created heated arguments among the parties concerned for over a year. Discussions were carried out primarily in the Education Promotion Council, the Conference of Presidents of National Universities and in the drafting committee for the University Supervision Law.

There was great variance between the opinions held by SCAP and by the university authorities. The fact that some universities had a long historical background and high academic standing while others had little background and comparatively low academic standing made it more difficult for the various groups to come to terms. After long deliberation a plan was worked out and submitted to the Diet, where legislation is still pending.

Reorganization of the Education Ministry

The Education Ministry was reorganized in May 1949 in accordance with the provisions of the Education Ministry Establishment Law (revised June 1952). The fundamental character of the Education Ministry as laid down in the Board of Education Law, Private School Law and other legislation was finally synthesized in the Education Ministry Establishment Law. The law provides that:

—Emphasis on administration of education shall be diverted from the practices of arbitrary orders and compulsory supervision backed by the power of the state and shall be centered in the principle of guidance and advice based on study, technical knowledge and experience.

—The system of education shall be decentralized and the principle of local autonomy shall be put into practice.

—Minimum standards shall be set for a democratic educational system and for the improvement and encouragement of the arts, science and culture.

—Research shall be undertaken and statistics prepared for use of individuals in science, art and cultural fields.

—Efforts shall be directed toward the enactment of laws necessary for the elevation of education, culture and science and toward the encouragement of financial aid and the procurement of reference materials.

In order to carry out the program outlined above, provisions are made for setting up a Central Education Council composed of fifteen members of a high degree of professional standing and long experience. This group is to advise the Minister of Education on matters of fundamental importance, after dissolution of the Educational Promotion Council.

V. Improvement in the Content and Methods of Education— Emphasis on Personality and Individuality

The guiding principles of Japanese education cover the entire field of education including the matter of setting the curriculum and its content. Consequently, a fundamental reform of the principles of education necessitates fundamental changes in the curriculum and its content. The former nationalistic compulsory education was centered on text books selected by the state. Text books selected by the state are generally used in moulding a uniform curriculum to meet the objectives and needs of the state, but neglecting the will of the individual. Teachers made state-chosen texts the only basis for teaching and faithfully followed state-designated policies, giving no attention to the personality and ability of the individual student.

The new concept of education aims at developing the individual's character and abilities by encouraging him to develop his own latent qualities. In order to do this, it is necessary to seek out and emphasize the potential powers, inclinations and interests within the individual. It is therefore desirable that in the educational guidance of an individual special attention be paid to his character and to the environment in which he was raised. From this point of view, it is desirable that the teacher prepare his own curriculum on the basis of conditions that he finds before him. Many teachers who were products of the old-style education did not have the experience or training to participate in such a program.

The Education Ministry therefore prepared a guide book on curriculum, after consultation with various experts. The guide sets standards of curriculum for the teachers to keep in mind when making plans for their own students.

Principles to Guide Studies

The guide book lays out the following basis for preparing a curriculum:

—A small number of broad subjects shall be prepared instead of a great number of many narrow sujects. For example, ethics, history, and geography in primary school and junior high school have now been revamped and unified under the single heading of *social studies*. This makes it possible to correlate the material and apply it directly to social problems.

—In junior and senior high schools the curriculum shall consist of required and elective subjects. Especially in senior high school a student may study a particular division of a larger subject, according to his own choice and based upon his ability, personality and interests.

—In order to improve study undertaken by the student on his own initiative in primary and junior high schools, there shall be hours of free study or hours of special study which are not designated as any particular subject.

—It shall be emphasized that studies shall be carried out to meet the needs of the particular community in a region where the school is located. Teaching materials will also be selected from those actually existing in that locality.

—Emphasis shall be placed on health education using many materials to teach the subject. Team games shall be stressed instead of martial training prevalent in prewar days.

—Domestic science courses have been established for fifth and sixth-grade primary school students, both male and female, where they study domestic affairs three hours each week. In the secondary schools, vocational and domestic science courses have been established as required study. This is aimed at giving the student the technical training and knowledge that is fundamentally necessary for maintaining a family and choosing a profession in keeping with his own interests and abilities.

Problems of Teaching Methods

After the courses have been reformed, there arises the question of how to teach the student the content of the new course. As already outlined, prewar primary school teaching methods were based on the nationwide use of a common text prepared by the Education Ministry allowing the student little latitude. Few teachers ever tried to digress from this rigid system to embark on advanced educational techniques.

After the end of the war, the prewar text books for teachers were replaced by a guide book for courses of study issued by the Education Ministry. In this guide book the American method of guiding children was introduced and it had a tremendous effect upon teaching methods in postwar Japan. The most conspicuous effects are:

—The attitude of the teacher toward the student has changed. Instead of doling out specific materials in a course, the teacher encourages the students to study under their own initiative and guides them in their work.

—The problem method, project method, discussion method and group discussion have been introduced into Japan for the first time.

—Visual and auditory aids have been introduced and encouraged in the school and class libraries in order to stimulate student interest in study.

—Attention has been directed toward the development of the talents of individual students on the basis of observation made of them.

Teaching methods have thus been changed from those where the teacher had played the leading role to those where the student now plays the leading role in the studies. This principle, however, is often misunderstood or superficially understood with the result of creating undisciplined students.

—The judgment of the results of education brings to the fore the question of "appraisal." In the past "evaluation" was used in the narrow sense of the word, taking it as the result shown in the marks attained by students in their courses at the end of the school term or school year.

Since the introduction of the new system of education, emphasis has been placed on understanding the student as an integrated individual. Not only his intellectual capacity but also his character, attitudes, physical and vocational skills are taken into consideration before appraisal is passed on 'he overall results of his education.

Reform of Text Books

Along with the improvements in the basic concepts of education, the curricula and the teaching methods, the role of the text book has decreased in importance. Since 1902 when the text book system was established in Japan, the text book had been regarded as the foundation of compulsory eduction and it was believed absolutely necessary for the student to assimilate the contents of the basic text. In the new education system, however, such overly uniform education has been discarded. The teachers have a free choice of materials and methods of teaching in order to best fit the course of study to the student's individual traits and best prepare him for life in his community.

With these changes in education, it has become necessary to re-vamp text materials in most courses and to change fundamentally the concept of having a single Education Ministry-prepared text book for each course. The new concept of the text book is that although it is the most important part of the teaching materials and lays out the pattern of systematized teaching, it is not the only material used in the course. The text book is now selected from many texts in order to best meet the interests and attitudes of the children as well as satisfy the needs of the community in which they live. It is augmented by several other types of teaching and reference materials. Keeping the above principles in mind, the Education Ministry prepared a set of model text books for students of primary schools and junior and senior high schools in 1947. The text book system underwent basic changes in 1948, and since 1949 text books prepared by private groups outside the Education Ministry have come into use. These are passed on by the Inspection Committee of the Education Ministry. At present a wide variety of approved texts are available, and teachers are permitted to make their selections from them.

Reforms of Promotion and Admission System

In keeping with changes in teaching methods and curricula, the system of admission to higher schools has been redrawn. The selection of a student for admission to senior high school is now made on the basis of a report prepared by the junior high school from which the candidate has graduated and an entrance examination. The examination is designed to measure the student's fundamental knowledge of particular subjects.

Admission to the university is based on a report from the senior high school, an entrance examination and a physical examination. The senior high school report is to be prepared objectively at a conference of teachers who were responsible for the student's senior high school education on the basis of the student's guidance records. The report has a fixed form. Physical examinations for applicants to national universities have been in use since 1948 when a system patterned on that used in the United States was instituted. The entrance examination tests the student's grasp of basic principles and his ability to apply them to particular situations. The examination questions are prepared on the basis of a careful study of the senior high school curriculum. Care is taken not to frame such question for admission that might cause an unhealthy influence on the sound development of high school education. The subjects of the examination are limited to the Japanese language, social studies, mathematics, science and foreign language. Some variations are found according to the specialization of the particular university.

VI. Has the New Educational System Actually Been Put into Practice? What is the Situation Today and What Are the Problems?

While the idea of educational reform has been given high praise, the actual enforcement of the new system is often far from **satisfactory**. The reason for this is that the reform, which might **take at** least ten years under normal conditions, has been carried **out in** Japan in a very brief period under very difficult political, **financial** and social conditions resulting from defeat in the war. The **following** three points are generally pointed to as unsatisfactory:

1) No yearly detailed plan was established when the system **was** initiated.

2) No sufficient financial provisions were made for its **enforce-** ment.

3) The re-orientation of teachers was not able to keep **pace with** the program.

Most of the disappointments and criticisms met while the **new** system was being put into practice were due mainly to **the above** causes. Actual conditions found today are outlined below.

Primary Schools

Although there was no change in the primary school **system,** primary school education has undergone remarkable changes **in study** materials and teaching methods. There were many cases **where** classes of the new junior high schools were established in **the same** school buildings as existing primary schools. In some cases, **school** buildings for the new junior high schools were built out of **a tight** budget, thereby necessitating delays in rehabilitation of war-**damaged** primary school buildings. This has caused a scarcity of **classrooms** for primary school children. Accordingly, in April 1951 there **were** inadequate classrooms for 20,314 classes, or eight per cent **of the** total number of classrooms in Japan. These inadequate **rooms were** temporary rooms without proper furniture, or classes that **were split** into morning and afternoon shifts because of overcrowding.

Junior High Schools

The new junior high schools were instituted in May **1947 in** compliance with the School Education Law of March of **the same** year. It was absolutely impossible to make the necessary preparations for such a fundamental change in schools and education in such a short time. In addition, the then prevailing political confusion, economic hardships and social unrest coupled with a transportation system that had almost been obliterated by air raids made it next to impossible to carry out investigations of the actual conditions of schools that had been damaged during the war. Accordingly, statistics could be obtained only for the number of students who had gone to remote rural areas to escape air raids, the number of school rooms lacking and the condition of those remaining and the whereabouts of the licensed teachers.

Short finances and lack of materials were such a great handicap that it was almost impossible to undertake the construction and rehabilitation of school buildings. These difficult situations were repeatedly brought to the attention of the Diet and SCAP and often created heated political discussions.

It was only in the 1952 fiscal year that the wholehearted support of public opinion and the Civil Information and Education Section of SCAP, made it possible to squeeze through an allocation of expenditures for construction or repair of school buildings to meet the minimum requirements. Expenses for establishment of schools for compulsory education, i.e., primary and junior high schools, are equally borne by the national government and the local autonomous bodies concerned. Actually, however, this principle has not been followed in practice because of meager budget allocations for education. As a result, parents of students have made great monetary contributions for construction and repairing of facilities, installation of teaching materials and meeting other needs of the schools. Originally, the Education Ministry maintained that it was reasonable and practical to convert sixty per cent of the then existing five-year middle schools and secondary grade vocational schools into the new three-year junior high schools which had been provided for in the new school laws. The majority of the five-year middle schools strongly opposed the conversion and created a great deal of confusion. The confusion was intensified by the shortage of teachers which resulted from the increase in the number of secondary schools.

The new school system got off to a poor start and confusion resulted from its hasty enforcement, but the situation has gradually improved. As of April 1951, there were 5,127,927 students and 191,615 teachers in the 12,328 junior high schools throughout the country. However, about twenty-one per cent of the teachers do not have proper qualifications and it is to be assumed that their teaching and guidance of school children may in many cases be less than satisfactory.

Senior high Schools

The senior high school system has been in effect throughout the country since 1948, a majority of them having been converted from the old-system middle schools. In the first year the number of schools reached 3,210, but this was reduced by 300 in later years due to reorganization and consolidation. In accordance with the Board of Education Law, the school district system is in use for the senior high school students. The establishment of senior high schools with a variety of vocational subjects has also been encouraged. This encouragement in some cases resulted in the consolidation of several senior high schools, paying no attention to the differences in historical, traditional or geographical backgrounds of the individual schools. There are now many elective subjects available to the student, according to his own interests in order for him to develop his own skills. The selection of courses is often not made profitably, due mostly to the lack of adequate guidance by the teachers.

Special evening senior high school courses of four years have also been established for young men and women who are financially unable to attend the regular senior high schools.

As of April 1921, there were 2,190,992 students and 110,482 teachers in the 2,963 senior high schools of Japan. Of the teachers, 6.1 per cent are not fully qualified.

Universities

Before approving the establishment of any university, the School Education Law states that the supervising authority (Education Ministry) must obtain the views of the University Establishment Committee. At the end of 1947 the University Establishment Committee (now the University Establishment Council) was set up with thirty-three members from organs of higher education, seven government officials and five members who were drawn from experienced and well-informed persons. This committee is responsible for investigation of schools that apply to elevate their status to the university level. After the result of the investigation is reported to the Education Ministry, the Ministry can approve or deny the application on the basis of the committee's recommendation, which in turn is based on established university standards.

Institutions for higher education have been concentrated in urban areas. In 1947 out of a total of 59 national, public and private universities of the old system and 90,000 students, the city of Tokyo had 28 universities and 49,000 students. Also in 1947, out of 655 universities, colleges, high schools and normal schools with 470,000 students, the three major cities of Japan—Tokyo, Kyoto and Osaka—had 257 schools and 254,000 students.

In order to improve this situation, the Education Ministry laid out a plan to set up at least one university in each prefecture. In May 1949, 267 nationally-supported colleges were reorganized into 69 universities under the new system. Twelve private and public colleges converted themselves into new-system universities in March 1948. The number has increased and as of April 1951 there were 283,975 male students, 29,183 female students and 23,280 teachers in the nation's 71 national, 26 public and 106 private universities.

Some results of the rapidly expanding university system have been unfavorable. First, the quality of professors has been lowered. The universities have been established without proper financial backing in the confusion of the postwar years. Consequently some of the universities are poorly built, poorly equipped and staffed with sub-standard teachers. Some national universities of different standards and qualifications and those in remote areas have been consolidated into one university. This has made it difficult for the university authorities to manage the schools on an efficient basis. The fact that, due to the strong recommendation of SCAP, the universities under the new system were established two years before the junior colleges has had an unhealthy effect on the sound development of the university system.

The necessity for speedy establishment of junior colleges was fully realized by the Education Ministry and Japanese educators, but their repeated appeals to SCAP for earlier establishment of the junior colleges were in vain. The establishment of junior colleges was not approved by SCAP until 1949, after the studies concerning the establishment of universities was completed.

The University Establishment Committee carried out investigations in the spring of 1948 to determine the future of a group of colleges, most of them private and one half of them women's colleges. Disapproval meant closure. Members of the committee were well aware of the historical backgrounds and merits of these colleges in serving the expansion of higher education. Therefore they sympathetically applied the required standards for universities. Consequently, the committee's generosity in their investigations set a bad precedent and resulted in the setting up of universities of lower standards.

In short, it may well be said that the standards of universities under the new system is below that of the universities of the old system. On the other hand, the present standard is higher than the old college standards. These results had been expected from the beginning. It is now expected that the standards will be raised as the universities continue their efforts, picking up appropriate financial aid and adequate personnel along the way. In spite of some failures and unfortunate circumstances, it is gratifying to note that the younger generation in the rural areas is being given much broader opportunities to acquire higher education. Continuing efforts will make the new system more effective and successful in the future.

Junior Colleges

Junior colleges are institutions to fill the gap between the four-year universities and the senior high schools, especially in the case of women. There were some private colleges under the old system which, although they failed to pass inspection by the University Establishment Committee, were of much higher standards than the senior high shools of the new system. The necessity for the establishment of junior colleges to deal with the situation was strongly recommended by the parties concerned. Temporary approval was granted in June 1949.

Authorization for establishment of junior colleges is granted by the University Establishment Committee. The requirements for teachers and students is the same as that of the universities. The first junior college was established in 1950 and by April 1951, there were 36,331 students with 6,554 teachers in 180 junior colleges. Of these, 152 were private. It is assumed that this will help popularize higher education, but it is too early yet to assess the results.

Medical and Dental Colleges

The exceptions to the four-year university course in this country are the medical and dental colleges. In prewar Japan, medical education was carried out in colleges and schools. Medical colleges admitted high school graduates to four years of studies solely in medicine. Medical schools offered four or five year medical courses to graduates of the old-system secondary schools. Dental schools usually gave four years of training after secondary school. Graduates of such medical and dental institutions were given licenses to practice without state examinations.

In 1946 it was decided that the education of doctors should be undertaken only by medical colleges. On the basis of population and other factors, the number of doctors required in the country was calculated and the number of students in medical universities was reduced so that the requirement would be met in 1951. Based on the records, installations and equipment of the schools, the University Establishment Committee conducted investigations which led to either approval or dissolution of the then existing medical and dental institutions.

As of April 1951, there were 30 medical colleges (19 national, 17 public and four private) and four dental colleges (two national, one public and one private).

Colleges for Teachers

Colleges for teachers were established upon introduction of the new education system with the aim of training teachers to participate in the new program. Theretofore teachers had been educated in normal schools, women's normal schools and young men's normal schools. In the new system it was felt that teachers should be trained in a four-year college course. Each prefectural government accordingly established either an independent college for teachers or an education or science and culture department within the existing university in the prefecture. These facilities were to train teachers to work within the schools of the prefecture.

These institutions plan their own curricula in compliance with the provisions of the University Establishment Law and the Teachers License Law of May, 1949. The teachers license is awarded to graduates of these institutions. Licensed teachers should have as their qualifications a deep knowledge of human culture, detailed familiarity with the material in school courses they might teach and adequate knowledge of techniques used in guiding the mental and physical development of youngsters. It is extremely difficult, however, to meet the schools' needs for 50,000 new, highly-qualified teachers each year solely from the graduates of the four-year college courses. In order to alleviate the situation, special two-year teachers' courses have been instituted in the institutions, which enables graduates to obtain a secondary license. Holders of secondary licenses are issued regular licenses when they are considered to be qualified by reason of their efforts to improve their techniques while serving as a teacher. Each year the national teachers colleges and universities expect to graduate 27,000 teachers from their two-year and four-year courses.

As of April 1951, there were fifty-two national and four public and private institutions with special two-year teachers courses. Most of these that are national colleges had been elevated from their former normal school status by reason of having improved their faculties and facilities. These normal schools, however, had rather sub-standard staffs and facilities, and it is felt that much improvement remains to be carried out. Consequently, these schools are considered the weakest point in the college and university setup in Japan.

Eligible teachers are given four different grades of licenses—first, second, temporary and extraordinary—in accordance with the kind of school they serve (primary, secondary, senior high or kindergarten), their status (teacher or assistant teacher), their professional classification (teacher, principal, guidance officer, or superintendent), and subjects they teach (standard Japanese language, social studies, physical education, etc.).

Post-Graduate Courses

Four private universities had post-graduate courses in 1950 and eleven in 1951. Post-graduate courses were first instituted in national universities in 1953, but the number will be limited.

VII. Problems to be Solved in the Future

The democratization of Japanese education after the war can be attributed mostly to the guidance and support of SCAP. However, SCAP made errors in some cases because it issued directives and pushed through programs without paying adequate attention to Japanese tradition and the actual social conditions found in Japan. Therefore, despite SCAP's good intentions, the result was that a number of unsolved problems are still found today.

One of these problems arose from the fact that SCAP put its

trust in school teachers to the extent of allowing them the power to strike. This has become a major source of trouble in postwar Japanese education. The Japan Teachers' Union should be held responsible for the neglect of its duties and responsibilities and for its betrayal of SCAP's trust. The Japanese people concerned are also to be held at fault because they failed to exert enough pressure to make SCAP change its policy on the teachers. Although nobody questions the good intentions of SCAP, it is felt that SCAP did not heed the appeals of informed Japanese at that time and forced through its decision without knowing all the facts in the case.

The reformation was carried out in such a short period of time without making appropriate preparations that it is quite natural that there remain some problems yet to be sloved.

There is now no complaint or opposition about the reformation of the fundamental principles of the education system. But it is urged that the new constitution for education be backed with a new set of philosophical principles.

From financial or emotional reasons, many advocated the reexamination of the new school system, and heated controversies developed. However, the overwhelming majority supported the new system, and, at least for the time being, criticism has subsided.

The formula of preparing curricula for primary and junior high schools on the basis of psychological factors and actual experience has been given overwhelming support. However, there are some who want a "more logical" formula to be added to the present courses.

The most controversial subject is social studies. There are many who insist that the history of a race or nation should not be taught under social studies. They also feel that it is necessary to add moral education to the practical guidance the students receive in order to help youngsters develop sound judgment. It is pointed out that this is particularly necessary because the influence of churches and Sunday schools is rather weak in Japan.

In teaching methods, teachers have been cautioned to be more active in urging students to be diligent in their duties, but not to smother the will of the child.

As for text books used in primary and junior high schools, it is advocated that the Education Ministry be more active and maintain higher standards of inspection of texts as well as of companies that publish them. The Education Ministry is also urged to maintain greater uniformity in the texts and to control overzealous sales competition among the numerous publishing houses.

It is being urged that the senior high school students' school districts be either changed or abolished depending on the actual conditions within the district concerned and also that the coordinated senior high school system be re-examined.

It is suggested that the number of elective subjects in senior high schools be reduced because of the sub-standard counseling of the teachers and the poor judgment and the lack of a will to study on the part of some of the students. It is further suggested that a few elective subjects be established that will help students toward entering higher educational levels or vocational fields.

At present a plan to set up a six-year senior high school, unifying the present junior and senior high schools, is under discussion.

Some quarters are advocating that three types of national colleges and universities be designated:

—Universities with graduate courses for those who will go on to advanced degrees.

—Colleges emphasizing vocational education.

—Colleges to train teachers.

It is feared that the American system of computing units will have harmful effects on Japanese education because the facilities of Japanese institutions of higher learning are poor by comparison.

In technical colleges—such as music, fine arts, etc.—it is generally felt that there are too many general subjects compared to the technical subjects, resulting in inadequate technical education.

Many private schools are advocating that the two-year pre-dental and pre-medical courses be made semi-independent.

There are two main points of view on the teachers' colleges. One group maintains that the two-year course is sufficient training for primary and junior high school teachers; the other maintains that a four-year course is absolutely necessary to bring teaching standards up to where they should be, although they recognize that the two-year course will be necessary for quite a long time as a temporary expedient.

Education circles urge the simplification of units in the teacher training curriculum required by the Teachers License Law.

National universities are being urged to try to make some of their departments particularly prominent in their own field, utilizing to the best advantage the school and the department's historical background, environment and past activities. It has also been urged that a way be opened for students to transfer from one university to another without loss of credit.

In order to further vocational education, it is urged that advanced vocational schools be formed by consolidation of senior high schools and junior colleges.

Because it is felt that students are victims of political, economic, social and ideological confusion, it is an urgent necessity that students receive guidance in living and welfare matters. In this connection, it is necessary to set up beneficial guiding principles and an effective organization. The Japan Association for Student Assistance should be expanded.

The purpose and status of post-graduate courses in the universities require study. The present post-graduate courses are merely an extension of undergraduate work and ill-suited to the present needs of a poor Japan. Former Education Minister Dr. Teiyu Amano and his many supporters have consistently urged that post-graduate work should be limited to a small number of selected scholars and research students and also as a place for refresher studies for those who have been away from the university for some time and have specific subject matters to study. They feel that in this way post-graduate institutions would be making a profitable contribution to the advancement of learning in the country. It is expected that the Education Ministry will lay down rigid requirements for the selection of those to be admitted to post-graduate studies.

In the course of the reform of the system of educational administration, decentralization has often been mistaken for democratization. The word *democratization* might be synonymous with *decentralization* in the United States, but in Japan it is necessary to make a clear distinction between the two words. Many people insisted on decentralization of educational administration because they feared that there would be a recurrence of the ultra-nationalistic tendencies prevalent in Japanese education after the outbreak of the Manchurian Incident. These people should keep in mind the feudal era when Japan was divided into almost three-hundred fiefs. Decentralization of administration of education has been carried too far, without paying due consideration to the historical background of the country and actual social conditions today. The Board of Education Law is a case in point.

In compliance with the law, in November 1952, 40,000 members were elected to 10,000 boards of education in cities, towns and villages throughout the country. By this action, a large number of people who were unqualified for the job were elected, thus adding unnecessary complexities to the problems of educational administration.

Therefore, it is expected that the time will soon come when it will be necessary to restudy :

—The local unit comprising a board.

—Method of selecting board members.

—Number of board members.

—Powers of the boards.

—Questions pertaining to educational financing.

—Relations between the boards and the Education Minister.

In regard to reorganization of the Education Ministry, it is pointed out that the power of the Education Minister is unduly restricted so that he cannot always respond to the will of the majority of the people. While the Education Minister is considered by the Diet and the nation as the person responsible for the educational administration of the country, his power is rigidly restricted by law. In other words, he is charged with the responsibility while his powers are strictly limited. The Education Ministry in Japan is different in character from the Office of Education of the United States government. It rather corresponds to the various state departments of education. The Education Ministry has changed from an administrative organ that once issued orders and carried out supervision backed by the strong power of the national government to an administrative organ whose main duties are guidance and assistance to educational institutions on technical, scientific and other pertinent matters. There is no reason, however, for the administrative relationship between the Education Ministry and the boards of education to remain severed by law as it is today. Rather it is necessary to establish a closer relationship between the two, in order to further the sound development of education in Japan. The Education Ministry should be the center of an organization of all the boards of education in the country, in order to achieve close coordination, guidance and mutual assistance among the boards.

Although the Education Minister has the responsibility of supervising all national universities, he has no administrative power over their personnel. This is left entirely in the hands of the respective universities, with decisions subject to review. Actually, the Education Minister does not even have veto power over the appointment or dismissal of university personnel. The same kind of relationship exists between the university presidents and the professors, or department heads and professors in the department. Therefore, it cannot be denied that the guarantees given to teaching status by the Law for Special Regulations concerning the Educational Public Service of January 1949 went too far and that the persons responsible for the overall supervision of education have not been given powers commensurate with their responsibilities. This has resulted in inequalities in personnel matters and a lack of competence in educational administration with the resultant unhealthy effects on the sound development of education.

In this regard, it is absolutely necessary that the Education Ministry as the central educational administrative agency be democratized to the fullest extent so that it can carry out its duties efficiently as an autonomous administrative body free from political influences. To serve this purpose, a Central Education Council has been set up within the Education Ministry as an advisory body to the Education Minister.

Generally speaking, in financially-pressed Japan, the democratization of education must be carried out on an efficient and simpler basis in order to reduce the economic burden on the nation. This point has not been adequately considered in the past. The plan for the establishment of various independent councils such as the Private University Council, Public University Council and the National University Council should be scrapped in favor of setting up one consolidated Central Council which would maintain closer coordination with the Central Education Council.

The reformation of the Japanese language, encouragement of social education, further promotion of science and culture and the improvement of educational finances are also problems that must be considered in the future.

THE POSTWAR ACTIVITIES OF THE JAPAN COMMUNIST PARTY

By Kinya Niiseki

Chief, 5th Section, European and American Affairs
Bureau, Ministry of Foreign Affairs

I.

At the end of World War II the international Communist movement's basic strategy was to hitch its wagon to democratic movements. The 7th general meeting of the Comintern, held in Moscow in July 1935, decided upon an "anti-Fascist united front." Accordingly, the Communist parties in various countries adopted the platform—"Down with Fascism"—and took up so-called people's front tactics. In a drastic party-line switch, the Communist parties soft-pedaled the class struggle against capitalism that they had spouted for years, and instead emphasized the necessity of protecting bourgeois democracy.

In individual countries, Communist parties built up united fronts by joining hands with many diverse groups, regardless of whether they were social democrats, liberals, racists, or even royalists. On the international level the movement culminated in World War II with the Allied Powers on one side, the Axis Nations on the other. When the Allies defeated the Axis nations of Japan, Germany and Italy, the international Communist movement discarded its negative and defensive tactics of anti-fascism, and adopted positive and offensive tactics based on the pretext of realizing democracy through the liquidation of remaining fascist influences.

Despite the fact that they were fundamentally different from other political parties, Communist parties attempted to come to power through the recognized channels of political democracy, by capturing a majority of seats in their respective national legislatures. At the same time the Communist parties decided to reorganize themselves into mass political parties and broaden their support by adopting a flexible platform that could be adjusted on occasion to particular national conditions. Because of lingering anti-Fascist sentiment, postwar economic problems, and political chaos, these tactics were fairly successful in several countries.

In general, the Japan Communist Party's actions after World War II followed the above-mentioned pattern. From 1922 when it was organized with the Comintern's help, the Japan Communist Party was persistently active until its total collapse in 1934. Its demise came about because of increasing pressure from the Japanese government and internal discord among its leadership. Some leaders who were arrested renounced their faith in communism; others sought refuge in overseas countries; those who remained loyal to the Comintern were all imprisoned. As a consequence, the Party history has a ten-year blank, and in Japan there was almost no organized resistance as in Europe, even after the outbreak of the Pacific War.

With the coming of the American occupation, the Peace Preservation Law and other thought-control regulations were annulled by virtue of the GHQ Memorandum of October 4, 1945 "regarding removal of restriction of political, civic and religious freedoms." Sixteen communist leaders including Kyuichi Tokuda, Yoshio Shiga and Kenji Miyamoto were released from prison. The Japan Communist Party was reorganized. The Party organ—*Akahata*—reappeared after an absence of eleven years, and the 4th general Party meeting was held—the first in the postwar period.

The reborn Party had lost all international connections because of the prolonged imprisonment of Tokuda and its other leaders. At first it had no choice but to resurrect the so-called "1932 thesis" handed down from the Comintern thirteen years earlier and swallow its antiquated contents as a basis for future policy. For example, a statement published on October 10, 1945, entitled "An Appeal to the People," reputedly written by Tokuda in prison, said: "Our target is to destroy the Emperor system and establish in its wake a people's democratic government based on the will of the people."

This statement revealed a marked theoretical disparity between Japanese communists and their colleagues in other countries. It gave priority to the overthrow of the Emperor system and relegated to second place the organization of a proletarian party with laborers and farmers as its nucleus. This directive was in extreme contrast to that of Chief Secretary Togliatti of the Italian Communist Party. Returning to Italy from the Soviet Union after the downfall of Mussolini in 1943, Togliatti persuaded other Italian political parties to abandon their precipitous demand for immediate abdication of the King. Instead he called for the building up of a united front of democratic influences, pointing out that it was an urgent necessity of the times.

Moreover, Japanese Communists grossly contradicted themselves, like true ultra-leftist tacticians, by urging farmers to refuse quota delivery of rice while engineering the "give-us-rice" demonstrations in cities. But these subversive activities only served to antagonize the people against Communism.

II.

Thus the Communist Party seemed to be in difficult circumstances when Sanzo Nosaka (alias Susumu Okano) returned home from Yenan, China after an exile of sixteen years. He was hailed as a "heroic savior of the country" when he landed in Japan in January 1946. The enthusiastic welcome given Nosaka closely resembled the frenzied reception accorded by the French people to Chief Secretary Thorez of the French Communist Party when he flew home from the Soviet Union in November 1944.

Unlike Tokuda and other Communist leaders who had spent many years in prison, Nosaka's long stay in Russia and Communist China made him well-versed in the tactics of the international communist movement. In fact, Nosaka had been a member of the Executive Committee of the Comintern until its dissolution in 1943. His return to Japan served to renovate the tactics of the Communist Party.

The Japan Communist Party owed its theoretical development chiefly to Nosaka until his theories were strongly censured by the Cominform in January 1950.

The most prominent characteristic of the Japan Communist Party's new strategy was its decision to adopt peaceful democratic methods in lieu of the formula of violent revolution advocated by the "1932 Thesis." Upon landing in his homeland, Nosaka's first words were, "Beloved Communists"—his newly coined motto. In the same breath he said, "The issue pivots on how violent revolution can be avoided. Certain people seem to interpret Leninism as synonymous with violent revolution, but they are wrong. The supposition that because Lenin and Stalin said such and such a thing Japan must also say it or do it is not the point. On the contrary, our starting point must be to determine the level of self-consciousness of the people and find out what the masses are thinking."

In regard to the Emperor system, Nosaka also took a moderate point of view—that its overthrow should be considered separately from the question of preservation of the Imperial family. At the same time he highly esteemed the role of the Occupation Forces in the cause of democracy. He declared, "The Occupation Forces are not here to make a colony of Japan," and apparently concluded that the presence of Allied forces was a favorable factor in the democratic revolution envisaged by the Communists. In short, the Japan Communist Party, under Nosaka's leadership, masqueraded as a real proletarian party determined to evolve a socialist system by peaceful and democratic methods under the American occupation. All this appeared quite consistent with the main current of Communist thought in Western Europe following World War II.

The new shift in strategy renewed the people's interest in the policies of the Communists whose popularity had been on the wane. As a consequence, in the first postwar general election of April 1946, the Communist Party won five seats in the House of Representatives, getting a total of 2,130,000 votes. It was the first time in Japan's history that the Communists had their voices heard in the Diet.

The most powerful group in the so-called "people's democratic front" of the Japan Communist Party was the trade union movement. The National Congress of Industrial Unions, which claimed 1,600,000 members, had been organized in August 1946 under the leadership of six regular Communist Party members and four secret party members and sympathizers. With the Congress under complete Communist control the Party took advantage of this favorable situation by persistently resorting to general strike tactics.

A big wave of labor trouble threatened Japan when an unprecedented general strike was suddenly declared involving 2,600,000 Government and public office employees. The date of the walkout was set for February 1, 1947. GHQ had been alerted to the dangers of extremist Communist agitation, however, and placed a ban on the strike. This showdown added to the rising tide of anti-Communist sentiment with the result that in the general election in April of the same year, the Communists mustered less than half the votes they had obtained in the preceding election.

With its general strike tactics stalemated, the Communists adopted a new tactic styled as "the people's area struggle." The area struggle was designed to have laborers join with farmers and townsmen in local struggles. They were instructed to make demands relating to living conditions and other problems in each geographical or industrial area, with the aim of eventually developing a nation-wide proletarian struggle. Wildcat strikes, desertion of shops and anti-tax disputes subsequently occurred everywhere in quick succession.

III.

From this point on, the Communist Party's attitude toward the Occupation underwent a gradual change. At its 6th general meeting held in December 1947, the Emperor "problem," the main theme of communist dogma in the past, was relegated to the background. A new slogan was brought to the front—"strict enforcement of the Potsdam Declaration." Though vaguely worded, this slogan was designed to initiate opposition to the Occupation. Its meaning differs greatly from the declaration of the Party's 4th general meeting which stated : " We should like to offer our deep thanks to the Allied Forces who, by occupying Japan, have paved the way for democratic revolution through the abolition of fascism and militarism."

This reversal of the Party line was not surprising. At that time the cold war between the United States and the Soviet Union was becoming increasingly bitter. In September 1947, the Cominform replaced the Comintern. Large-scale general strikes were going on in France and Italy, with the objective of opposing the Marshall Plan, or in plainer language the United States. To anyone familiar with these events, it is small wonder that the Japan Communist Party chose to reveal its pro-Soviet and anti-American nature at this time.

Then the Party added a new catchword—national independence—to its old slogans of " peace " and " democracy " and widely recommended establishment of a " democratic national front " in lieu of the " people's democratic front." About the same time the Party clarified its stand on the Japanese peace issue. It started beating the drum for an overall peace and against establishment of military bases in this country, as if in concert with the moves of the Soviet Union in international political circles. A movement opposing the so-called separate peace was launched.

Concurrently, the Communists focused their efforts on the then approaching general election campaign. They decided to exploit the election to break the stalemate resulting from the failure of the labor offensive. Accordingly, the Party cautioned its members against anarchistic or " wildcat " tendencies. It criticized such methods on the grounds that they would incite a chain of struggles and negate possibilities of a peaceful settlement. The Party took the position that revolutionary tactics are not merely headlong advances, uncompromising attitudes or strong offensives ; that in certain situations retreats or compromises are excellent tactics. Its leaders told the rank and file that " a general election is a struggle for political power."

In the general election of January 1949, the Communist Party won, relatively speaking, a signal victory surpassing all expectations. Thirty five of its candidates were elected and the total vote for the Communists was 2,980,000. Of the total, however, one half were marginal votes cast by people suffering from economic difficulties and disgusted with the corruption in political parties. In voting Communist, these people sought a panacea in the Party's cry for a " democratic national front."

At that time the overwhelming victory of the Communist army in China encouraged many Japanese Communists, and appraising the situation as especially favorable, Communist leaders began thinking in earnest of participation in political power. They took pains to broaden the scope of their democratic national front as much as possible and taking their cue from Communist China, they sought to enlist " national capitalists " in their own cause. They also pushed the overall peace and the Sino-Japanese trade movement more energetically than ever before. Meanwhile, they kept in readiness an organization called the " Democracy Defense League " as the seed of a Soviet regime for future Japan.

At the same time, the Communist Party launched its own membership drive to spread Communism among the Japanese under the slogan : " Acquire a million Bolsheviks!" Every one was welcome to join the Party as a regular member. Those were the days when Pastor Sakaye Akaiwa—a Protestant minister—and Professor Takashi Ide—a philosophy professor at Tokyo University—joined the party and the Zenshin theatrical troupe also entered it en masse. The Party, which on the day of its postwar reorganization claimed one thousand members, now reported a membership of 300,000.

Thinking that participation in the government was close at hand, the Communist Party made serious preparations for its anticipated new role. With regard to the feasibility of establishing a " people's regime " under the Occupation, Nosaka said : " Establishment of a people's regime depends on the support of the great majority of the people. The new situation in China may have a grave effect on relationships among the Allied Powers. Whether they like it or not, the Allies will have to recognize a government that is overwhelmingly supported by the vast majority of the people."

The Communist Party timetable for overthrowing the Yoshida cabinet was September 1949, and once again it built up a strong labor offensive. Under Party leadership a series of violent acts occurred, including the unauthorized operation of electric cars, the unlawful occupation of the Taira Police Station, the Mitaka electric car wreck, and the Matsukawa train wreck. Batches of ex-servicemen, detained and educated on Communist lines in the Soviet Union, just "happened" to return to Japan at this time. Their cry was, "We are effecting a landing on the Imperial Island in the face of the enemy," and they proceeded to riot and disturb the peace in different parts of the country. For a time it looked as if Japan were on the eve of a veritable revolution.

These violent and subversive activities engineered by egotistical Communists evoked bitter criticism from the people. Above all else, the indescribable language and behavior of the " Siberia repatriates " made the people suspect that they were deliberately working for the Kremlin. The Communist bandwagon for national independence occasioned serious misgivings among the people who became increasingly on guard against the doings of the Communist Party. As a result, the trade union movement which had been led by Communists became more moderate. As the " Democratization League " was ballyhooed, the influence of industrial unions declined, and its membership dwindled to 400,000—one fourth of its previous strength.

At this point Nosaka's theory of setting up a " people's regime " by means of his " peaceful revolution formula " fell apart. Disputes in the inner circles of the Communist Party became increasingly apparent.

IV.

In November 1949, the third Congress of the Cominform was held in Hungary. It passed a resolution stating that the principal mission of the Communist parties was to wage a struggle in the cause of peace. In plainer language, the point of this resolution was an extensive anti-American and anti-British campaign in the name of peace. Meeting at the same time as the Congress was the Conference of Asia-Pacific Area Trade Unions, affiliated with the Communist-dominated World Labor Federation. On the basis of a proposal introduced by Liu Shao Chi of the Chinese Communist Party, the Conference passed a resolution of great significance : that a people's emancipation army be organized under Communist leadership for the emancipation of Asiatic nations.

In early January 1950, the Cominform organ scathingly attacked Nosaka : "Nosaka's theory that the Japan Communist Party, even under the Occupation, could take over the government peacefully not only had nothing to do with Marx-Lenin-Stalinism, but reveals admiration of American imperialism."

Shaken by the Cominform's abrupt and relentless attack, Japanese Communist leaders had no alternative but to bow toward the Kremlin. They have since made withdrawal of U.S. armed forces their first order of business. Besides their legitimate activities in the Diet, they decided to mobilize proletarians and wage an anti-American struggle, even resorting to physical force. In late March 1950, the Communist Party organ "*Akahata*" published a statement of the Central Committee under the title, "An Appeal to the Entire Nation in the Interest of Our National Independence." It was almost unprecedented in its outspoken anti-American propaganda. Among other things, the article said that with Japan's economy completely under the control of foreign capital and her culture and education reduced to colonial standards, her whole territory was being converted into a military base for anti-Soviet activities.

Obviously, the Cominform's criticism of Nosaka's theory prompted a turn in the strategy of the Japan Communist Party. Its new tactics took form in the Eels episode when Tohoku and Hokkaido University students interfered with the lectures of an educational advisor to GHQ, SCAP, and the manhandling of American soldiers at the May Day rally in Tokyo. These incidents were on a small scale, but drew public attention as the first cases of their kind.

In connection with these demonstrations, GHQ on June 6 purged from public service 24 members of the Party's Central Committee. This drastic move dealt a near fatal blow to the Party leadership, including Tokuda and Nosaka. In a counter-move, the Party organized a Provisional Central Directorate in place of the Central Committee and chose Etsuro Shiino to head the new group. Seventeen staff members of the *Akahata*, the Party organ, were also purged, followed by a wholesale ban on the *Akahata* and about a thousand other Communist publications. Although the Party subsequently issued a journal called "In the Cause of Peace and Independence" and other illegal publications, the Occupation measures dealt the Communist structure some heavy and far-reaching blows.

In the labor field, the Communists also suffered a series of defeats. The Communistic National Liaison Council of Trade Unions (Zenroren) was ordered dissolved on August 30. The electrical industry, whose workers comprised a strong Communist element, and several other important enterprises enforced the so-called "red purge," firing Communists and Communist sympathizers in their employ. As of the end of 1950 more than ten thousand workers had been purged.

Communist Party influence has tapered off perceptibly as a result of the changing situation. According to official registration, figures, Party membership reached a peak of 100,000 in March 1950, but it dwindled gradually to 65,000 in January 1951, 59,000 in May, 56,000 in August and 48,000 in June 1952. Its actual strength, including nonregistered Communists, which was once thought to be 300,000 was recently estimated at 60,000 to 70,000. The number of members who are actually paying dues to the Party is said to be between 20,000 and 30,000 at most.

The yardstick of Party strength, however, is the quality and not the quantity of its members. Party membership which had increased 300 times in the short period of five years following World War II included much dead wood. A considerable number of opportunists had

joined Party ranks with the expectation of making a future for themselves. Many of these " fringers " promptly deserted the Party when
the strong policy of Occupation authorities and the government made
it uncomfortable to remain a member. The Party actually welcomed
the housecleaning as good riddance of rubbish.

The entire character of the Party changed from a predominantly
proletarian party to a vanguard for Bolshevist revolution. It was
apparent from the Constitution of the Japan Communist Party, adopted
at the 4th National Congress in February 1951, that the Party was
paving the way for unlawful activities by forming a strong proletarian
vanguard and screening its members more carefully. For example,
Article 7 of the Constitution stipulates : " (a) Members shall scrupulously
observe the provisions of the Constitution, and always be ready to
subject their private life to Party discipline ; (b) For the sake of the
Party and revolution, members shall protect necessary secrets at the
risk of their lives ; (c) Even in case of arrest, members should never
disclose matters concerning the organization of the Party.

It is, therefore, naive to hold the optimistic view that the
decrease in Party membership is an index of the grave blow the Party
has suffered. With the emphasis on underground activities, unlawful
actions by Communists have been greatly intensified of late. Communist leaders who have gone underground are incessantly contact-
ing their comrades at secret meeting places and via agents. They
are actually engaged in a type of guerilla activity.

V.

It is an indisputable fact that the Japanese nation has become
more critical, cautious and antagonistic toward the Communists. The
Communists themselves were not slow to recognize the disadvantages
of brandishing the old Communist banner, and gradually shifted their
tactics to flank movements. Now the Party has dropped the banner
of " socialist revolution " and has decided to appeal to Japanese
psychology with a new cry of " peace " and " independence."

The illegal Communist publication " *Naigai Hyoron* " (Domestic and Foreign Review), No. 26, August 23, 1951, published the new general principles of the Japan Communist Party. *Pravda*, official organ of the Soviet Communist Party, reproduced the article in full. This is evidence that the new program of the Communist Party in Japan has the Kremlin's blessing. Popularly called the 1951 Thesis, the new principles advocate formation of a league of farmers and laborers as a revolutionary force. The Thesis states, "Many entrepreneurs and big merchants as well as medium and small tradesmen suffering from the reactionary policy of the Yoshida government should join the league. All progressive elements should participate in it, regardless of their social position. Large and small progressive political parties and all progressive intellectuals should also take part in it."

The Party's new slogan is "democratic united front for emancipation of the people." The change from "people's democratic front" to "democratic national front" and then to the present slogan is a clear indication of the Party's alteration of tactics. The watchword "national independence" (opposition to U.S. influence), has gradually increased in weight over "freedom", and it is now the Party's main watchword.

Nosaka's theory that a people's regime could be established even under the Occupation, is from the Communist viewpoint erroneous. According to the Cominform decree, it flaunts the theory of International Communism which is dedicated to the protection of the Soviet Union International Communism's immediate objective in Japan is the anti-American struggle, and the fight against the government is part of the strategy. The new thesis defines the Yoshida government as "a spiritual and political bulwark of the American occupation." Therefore, the Communists' immediate aim must be to promote a broad united front against the United States in the name of a "democratic united front for national emancipation."

Socialistic policies held in common with the Communists, such as the nationalization of banks, big enterprises, land, etc., are to be utilized toward this end. For the present the goal of the Japan Communist Party shall be labelled "democratic revolution," not "socialist revolution."

The Party organ *Zenei* (Vanguard), No. 58, states: "For the sake of peace and independence, the urgent task of the working class in the current struggle is to stand at the head of the entire people's struggle, for over-all peace and withdrawal of all Occupation forces, and against rearmament. This struggle is the pivot of the class war at present."

The Party's illegal organ *Naigai Hyoron*, No. 27, states: "The Party will extend positive aid and cooperation to encourage not only workers but also farmers, entrepreneurs and merchants, who are suffering under the Occupation and the Yoshida government, to join with progressive influences in the united front for the emancipation of the people. It is even possible to induce big industrialists to favor neutrality by bringing them closer to anti-American and anti-traitor lines". Incongruously, the Party is trying to attract big capitalists to its anti-American line.

Recently, the Communists have shown a strong tendency towards taking anti-American utterances and actions of right-wing politicians and former career soldiers and turning them to their own use. In the peculiar atmosphere of April 1952 when Japan regained her independence after a seven-year occupation, it was not unexpected that anti-foreign incidents would occur from time to time. The Communists have proved adept at exploiting these incidents for propaganda purposes. We Japanese ought to be more wary of the Kremlin which is scheming to estrange this country from the Western camp by taking advantage of our national sentiment for complete independence.

The Communist Party of Western Germany, which stands on much the same footing as ours, adopted a thesis at its Central Committee's 18th general meeting in February 1951. The thesis is reputed to state: "Any split whatever in the enemy camp must be utilized to our benefit; if necessary, even compromise is permissible. Reactionary organizations which include laborers, farmers or intellectuals should be utilized. Remaining Nazis who are targets of the denazification program should also be utilized."

In Japan too there is a great possibility that extreme rightist elements may be used as pawns in the "democratic united front for emancipation of the people." It is noteworthy in this regard that the "Questions and Answers on Military Policy", approved at the 5th National Congress of the Japan Communist Party in October 1951, contains a passage saying, "For the benefit of the whole united front, we should extend a helping hand to the anticipated military moves of nationalists or adventurers."

A slogan which ranks with "peace" in the Communist Party is "national independence." Especially since the outbreak of the Korean war in June 1950, the "peace protection movement," with the Communist Party as its core, has been very active. It goes without saying that the movement constitutes a phase of the Kremlin's peace offensive. "Peace" is the most magic of all words to the Japanese, who experienced the misery and distress of war defeat for the first time, and moreover, were the first victims of the atomic bomb. For this reason the Communists are persistently hammering on their "peace movement" theme along with the tempting suggestion of unrestricted trade with Communist China. Their catchwords are "withdrawal of occupation forces," "opposition to military bases," and "anti-rearmament."

In 1951 and 1952, coincidental with this movement, Ikuo Oyama received the Stalin peace prize; Stalin delivered his peace statement to the Japanese people; and invitations were extended to Japanese nationals to attend the International Economic Conference in Moscow and the Asia-Pacific Peace Conference in Peking. Thus it can be seen that the Moscow-Peking peace offensive against Japan is being intensified.

VI.

Behind the scenes of the Communist peace movement, the groundwork is being laid for unlawful activity in the form of an "armed people's struggle." Under the title, "New Duties of Communists and Patriots...Fight Force with Force!", the *Naigai Hyoron* (Domestic and Foreign Review) of October 12, 1951 pointed out that armed masses are necessary to fight an armed foe. Communist China's armed intervention in the Korean War in November served to spur Japanese Communist preparations for armed struggle.

The Japan Communist Party's 4th National Congress in February 1951 adopted what was termed a "military policy." It was an epochal decision in the sense that the Party had been camouflaging its steady preparations for armed revolution by a sham peace movement.

This military policy is set forth as follows:

"The Japanese people are being controlled by American imperialism and its reactionary Japanese agents such as bankers, landowners and bureaucrats. This control is being maintained through the combined efforts of all terror groups such as domestic mercenary troops, the police, and bands of believers in club-law, with the American Army as the main force. Revolution therefore requires a people's armed struggle forceful enough to drive off the American army and smash all pressure machinery which have recourse to force. Under such conditions, the war for emancipation of the people shall be carried out by armed uprisings and general strikes of the working classes as soon as certain subjective and objective conditions are fulfilled."

The activities of pro-Communist Korean residents in Japan are noteworthy as they represent one aspect of the Communist Party's unlawful maneuvers. Some groups of Koreans in this country were in very close relationship with the postwar Japan Communist Party. In 1946 the Party issued a statement which read: "Without liberation of Korea there will be no revolution in Japan, and without revolution in Japan there will be no liberation of Korea." Korea's Kim Chyon Hai was a member of the Party's Central Committee and its Political Bureau. The Korean Residents League (Choren), formed in October 1945, was totally under Communist control. The Japanese government ordered the League dissolved in September 1949 on grounds of illegal activities.

An underground structure was soon formed to conduct clandestine activities, and a series of serious and lesser riots broke out all over the country after the outbreak of the Korean War. According to a report issued by the Judicial Committe of the House of Representatives in February 1951, the riots were "joint products of North Korean believers in club-law and Communists," who decided to act in concert with the Korean outbreak and to block cooperation between the Japanese government and the United Nations Command.

Duly registered Koreans under Communist influence in this country number 460,000 or 80% of all Korean residents. With unregistered residents and illegal entrants taken into account, the total number exceeds 600,000. Of this figure 1,500 are registered members of the Japan Communist Party; with Korean Communist sympathizers included the number would be about 100,000. These Koreans established and maintain an illegal organ called the "Fatherland Defense Committee." Its main objectives are to hinder production of war supplies, block transportation, spy on United Nations military bases, and do everything to disturb internal peace and order. In most of the recent riots in Japan, there were Koreans behind the scenes who are called "parachutists of the Communist army."

Koreans played an important role in the May Day turbulence that occurred in Tokyo's Imperial Palace Plaza on May 1, 1952, less than one month after independence was restored to Japan. From the standpoint of the number of participants and the ferocity of the rioters, the disturbance was unprecedented in scale. 740 police officers were seriously or slightly wounded; four foreigners were injured; 42 Japanese or foreign-owned automobiles were damaged or burned. Casualties on the Communist side included one dead, seven missing and 450 serious or slight injuries, according to a statement issued by the Party. On May 30, police stations in various parts of Tokyo were attacked by mobs. On June 25, the second anniversary of the outbreak of the Korean war, bamboo spears, flame throwers, oil or vitriol and gas bombs were widely used in riots in Tokyo and Osaka.

Japan has no monopoly on such disturbances, however. On May 11 an incident of like nature occurred at Essen, West Germany, and on the 28th of the same month another in Paris. In both incidents rioters collided with the police, and many casualties were reported. It should be noted that these riots took place almost simultaneously in the East and the West. The timing coupled with the similarity in techniques made people suspect that directives from behind the Iron Curtain were responsible.

The most common feature of these incidents was that participants in all disturbances were not workers but undisciplined mobs. In Japan the participants were mostly Korean Communists, students, and day-laborers—people with no direct social responsibility. Few trade union members of important enterprises were found among the rioters.

In summary, none of these incidents happened suddenly as a reaction to acute social or economic conditions, but were instigated by the Communist Party. Losing its grip over the majority of labor, the Party was working desperately under external pressure to arouse confusion in the minds of the people by mobilizing a handful of extremists to stage the riots.

Shortly afterward a Cominform organ dated July 1 printed an article entitled "On the Thirtieth Anniversary of Establishment of the Japan Communist Party." The author of the article was Kyuichi Tokuda, Secretary-General of the Japan Communist Party. He warned his comrades against conducting any unlawful struggle that was meaningless. He wrote: "Leaders who are devoting too much energy to strikes or demonstrations often neglect other forms of struggle such as elections for the Diet or local administrative and legislative organs. Our duty is to keep the people's trust by mastering the art of combining legal activities with illegal ones."

Taking its cue from Tokuda, the *Akahata*, dated July 15, printed an article in the name of the Central Directorate of the Communist Party. Its title was "Priority in Current Struggles," and it stressed that "making light of election struggles was a betrayal of class war."

As a result of this self-criticism the "Molotov cocktail" tactics then in vogue were suddenly abandoned for legitimate activities. In reality, the Party switched its strategy in view of the approaching general election.

On October 1, 1952, a general election was held after a lapse of nearly four years. The Communist Party campaigned strenuously, putting up one candidate for each constituency throughout the country, but failed miserably. Whereas 35 Communist candidates had been successful in the preceding election, not a single seat was won by the Communist Party in the new House of Representatives. The aggregate Communist vote also dropped from 2,980,000 (9.7%) in the preceding general election to 890,000 (2.5%) in 1952 election.

The Communists' disastrous defeat in this election was due partly to the fact that Tokuda, Nosaka and other well-known leaders had gone underground and the Party had been forced to sponsor candidates who were relatively less well known. The greatest cause of their failure, however, was the people's antipathy toward the Communists, particularly their violent "Molotov cocktail" tactics. The Soviet Union's cool attitude toward the question of admitting Japan to the United Nations and also to that of war prisoners added to Japanese distrust of Soviet policy, despite the Soviet's peaceful gestures toward Japan. All these factors apparently combined to influence the voters against the Communist Party.

In the April 19, 1953 general election, the number of Communist votes decreased to 660,000 (1.89% of the total votes cast) and the Communist Party barely managed to win one seat in the House of Representatives, reflecting the general ill-feeling of the public toward the party.

It would be premature, however, to conclude that the disastrous defeats suffered by the Communist Party in the 1952 and 1953 general elections have resulted in an elimination of Communist influence in Japan. The fact remains that the Communist Party, in spite of public antipathy, acquired more than 600,000 votes in both elections, and that, with the help of a large majority of some 600,000 Korean residents who are Communists or pro-Communists (as aliens they have no vote), it can reasonably be estimated that at least 1,300,000 people in Japan would support its destructive activities in the event of an emergency.

VII.

Since the April 1953 general election, the Communist Party pushed forth its struggle for power under the slogan of " anti-Yoshida, anti-rearmament, and establishment of a united government under the Communist Party." This policy, however, proved to be a clear failure, exposing the complacency and over-optimistism of the Communist leaders in judging the public feeling.

The Japanese people in general have gradually regained, with the progress of the economic rehabilitation and stabilization program of the government, their normal psychological bearings. Many who once were attracted to the Communist Party have sobered up and frown on its policy of violence.

Compelled to restudy its policy, the Communist Party finally adopted an " Interim Platform " towards the end of October or the beginning of November 1953.

In this Platform, the Communist Party frankly admitted that the balance of power between the two worlds was unfavorable to the Communist camp, and made it plain that the main objective of the Party " should be to increase Communist strength by strengthening the Communist Party, the National Liberation Front and the Democratic United Front."

In order to attain this objective and to rally the public to the united front of " anti-America, anti-Yoshida and anti-rearmament," the Communist Party proclaimed two platforms, one aimed at speeding up the unification movements for the " protection " of peace and democracy and the other, at inducing the public to recognize that a united front is necessary for the protection of their basic right to a decent living. The Party also pointed out the following nine items as measures for attaining the objective:

1.   Opposition to San Francisco Peace Treaty and Japan-U.S. Security Treaty, to conclusion of MSA agreement and to U.S. interference in domestic affairs.

2.   Opposition to foreign military bases; withdrawal of foreign troops.

3.   Restoration and adjustment of just and fair relations with all countries, including Soviet Union and Communist China; revival of free trade on basis of equality and reciprocity; opposition to international trade under unilateral U.S. control.

4.   Freedom of travel to foreign countries (meaning to Iron Curtain countries).

5.   Opposition to militarization of industry; guarantee of peaceful development of industry.

6.   Freedom of speech, assembly and association; complete guarantee of people's democratic rights.

7.   Opposition to revival of militarism and to mercenary armed forces of U.S.

8.   Opposition to Pacific military alliance and all other aggressive military alliances under any name.

9.   Overthrow of Yoshida government.

It should be noted that although the new policy may appear at first sight to constitute a retreating tactics, it is actually a clear tactical advance.   The Party has switched from its unrealistic tactics of " anti-America, anti-Yoshida and establishment of a united government under the Communist Party " to the more realistic tactics of strengthening the " anti-American and anti-Yoshida united front " as the prerequisite for attaining its objective.

At the same time, the fundamental policy of armed struggle has never been given up by the Communist Party, and the program for strengthening and arming of the " nuclear self-defense corps " is apparently being carried out relentlessly.   The Party has given careful attention to the operation of its military organizations so as to prevent them from going too far ahead of the masses and to concentrate, at least for the time being, on the military training of members of·the corps and their military leaders as well as on the education of the public on the necessity of armed struggle.

In accordance with the new policy mentioned above, the Communist Party is said to have already approached the left-wing Socialist Party with a proposal for a united front and started its campaign to win the support of the labor groups connected with that Party. The persistent moves of the Communist Party to regain popular support require careful watching.

JAPAN'S LABOR MOVEMENT

By Ichiro Nakayama

Chairman, Central Labor Relations Board
President, Hitotsubashi University

Introduction

In Japan's defeat in World War II were hidden the seeds for regeneration of its defunct labor movement. The liberal Trade Union Law, passed by the Diet on December 22, 1945, gave new impetus to dormant labor forces which expanded remarkably in a very brief period.

Trade unions had existed in Japan before the war and at times their activities had attracted nation-wide attention. The labor movement was the natural consequence of Japan's economic development along capitalistic patterns. After World War I the movement gained considerable momentum. Records for 1929 reveal 330,000 members in 630 unions, with 1,420 labor disputes during the year. In those days, however, Japan had no trade union laws and unions came under the jurisdiction of the Association Control Law as did all other organizations. Consequently, compared to postwar unionism the prewar labor movement had little magnitude and far less social significance. The advent of the Trade Union Law brought about a radical change, bestowing on the trade union movement an unusually advanced charter on which to base its development. The following chart, based on data from the Statistics Research Division of the Ministry of Labor, illustrates the rapid growth of unions after the war.

Year	Number of Unions	Total Membership	Percentage of Labor Organized
1946	11,579	3,748,952	40.0
1947	23,323	5,692,179	46.8
1948	33,926	6,677,427	54.3
1949	34,688	6,655,483	55.7
1950	29,144	5,773,908	45.9
1951	27,644	5,686,774	42.6
1952	27,851	5,719,560	40.2
1953	30,129	5,842,678	40.9

* All figures as of June of the year.

The strength of the union movement is not necessarily reflected in the percentage of organized labor. This is particularly true in Japan where in a short time the percentage of labor organized reached the level of Great Britain and far surpassed that of the United States. In appraising the strength of the Japanese labor movement, it must be kept in mind that this extremely rapid growth took place during the economic upheaval of the postwar period and under the sponsorship of the U. S. Occupation. The fact that the percentage of organization, which at one time reached 57 per cent, has recently fallen by some 20 per cent seems to indicate that the unnatural :expansion of those days is undergoing a readjustment. However, no intelligent person will deny the momentous fact that Japan's postwar labor movement has broken through the old institutional structure. Its rapid growth is calling upon the economic world to rewrite its charter anew. Thoroughgoing democratization of Japan was the basic stipulation of the Potsdam Declaration. Judging from the results, the development of trade unions and the completion of the agricultural land reform program are expected to have great and long-lasting influence on Japan, particularly in the economic sphere.

Principal Problems

What were, then, the principal problems posed by Japanese trade unions which had developed so rapidly? There were three principal problems—the problem of wages from the economic viewpoint, the problem of labor contracts from the legal viewpoint, and the problem of organization from the standpoint of the development of trade unions.

First, the pressing problem was wages which had not kept pace with a galloping inflation that spiraled upward for four years after the end of the war. Newly formed unions devoted themselves to an all-out struggle to raise wages in order to protect the workers' living standards from the rampant inflation. A fair appraisal of the situation would be impossible without some knowledge of the background of the struggle. In the three years of 1946–1947, 1947–1948, 1948–1949 commodity prices multiplied by four, three and two times respectively. The target of union struggles was the winning of a high enough wage to safeguard the minimum standard of living.

Although they could not justify their demands in theory, they gauged their repeated demands for higher and higher wages on climbing price indices of consumer goods. In the two inflationary years of 1947 and 1948 there were a total of 1,035 and 1,517 labor disputes, 80 per cent of which were related to wages and allowances.

This situation requires no special explanation as it is nothing more than a more severe and broader reenactment of the struggle of wages against rising prices found everywhere in the world. However, the case in Japan had one important peculiarity. In Japan the labor disputes which centered on higher wages were interwoven with a spontaneous demand for democratization of management. This ushered in a peculiar labor tactic known as "production control." Production control means that during a labor dispute the trade union temporarily takes over the management of the company or factory concerned. This dealt a serious blow to management, which was quite unable to cope with the rapidly changing situation. From January to August 1946, there were 137 cases of labor disputes involving production control—an indication of the rapidity with which this new tactic developed.

Inflation in Japan, which began to level off toward the close of 1948, practically came to a halt in 1949 as the result of the implementation of the "Dodge Plan." But trade unions continued to make strong demands for higher wages, and the number of disputes due to such demands did not decrease perceptibly. The principal cause for this was that even as late as 1952 the wages of Japanese workers —except for a few—had not reached prewar averages. Even after the halt of inflation, there was a vigorous movement to restore wages to at least prewar levels. The revival of inflationary tendencies that followed the outbreak of the Korean war in June 1950 gave new impetus to the demands for higher wages. However, trade unions in large enterprises had already achieved wages equal to prewar levels. The fact that such unions were the most influential in leading the struggle for higher wages raised some problems. "Sohyo" (General Congress of Japanese Trade Unions) has recently switched from demands based on "living security" to those based on "theoretical cost of living" in an effort to find a way out of this dilemma.

The second problem is that of the labor contract. Generally speaking, a labor contract is a concrete expression of labor-management relations in existence at a certain time. This is also true in the case of Japan; the contents of a labor contract will reveal the changing conditions of the Japanese labor movement. In the days following the immediate postwar reopening of the labor movement, newly organized unions—almost without exception—demanded the signing of a labor contract. By so doing, their prime purpose was to secure the fundamental right of labor to work. For some time employers not only lacked the power to resist such demands, but also thought it useless to refuse because the proposed terms were mainly of an abstract nature. Labor contracts were thus concluded between management and local units of the unions as well as with federations of unions. But the attitude of employers toward contracts began to change at the end of 1947, bringing with it a reaction from the unions. The employers' attitude began to change as they gradually began to recover prestige, and they began to insist upon their rights of management as opposed to the unilateral demands made by the labor unions. The unions have since lost some of their former enthusiasm for contracts because the benefits derived from a contract were not necessarily appreciated by a majority of the members and unions found it difficult to agree with management on clauses for settlements of grievances, which they were requested to insert in new contracts. (These clauses are known as "peace clauses" and "grievance remedy provisions.") Consequently, many unions went along without contracts until a kind of "no-contract era" developed by 1949. In order to remedy this situation, the Japanese government has exerted efforts to counsel the signing of contracts. Thus the records of 1952 show that about 60 per cent of the unions worked under contracts, but it is believed that the real figure is somewhat lower.

Early postwar labor contracts had many clauses governing personnel matters, unions claiming it their right to join with management in decisions on the hiring and firing of workers. In addition to these personnel clauses, unions also secured rights to participate in the actual management of the enterprise, resulting in the establishment of "management councils." Unions based these two types of demands on their basic right to work. Some current contracts still retain these types of provisions, but generally speaking the unions' unilateral demands for "the right to work" have become more moderate as management has regained its prerogatives.

Labor contracts signed since 1948 have clauses governing union shops, full-time union workers and non-union labor. Consequently, labor's demands for the right to work which were provided for only in abstract terms in earlier contracts, are now set down clearly in the new contracts. The problems of full-time union workers were more or less technical and settled without much difficulty. However, it was difficult to reach agreement on problems of union shops and non-union labor because the positions of management and labor were diametrically opposed. Both parties haggled over the issues involved so long that contracts expired, leading to the development of the so-called "no-contract era." Recently, however, both management and labor have given equal recognition to labor's right to work and management's right to manage. This has facilitated the solution of these problems and has resulted in a remarkable increase in the number of signed labor contracts. Among the big unions, in particular, almost all have written contracts. This new situation may be regarded as indicating a healthy growth in the Japanese labor movement.

The problem of trade union organization is so complex that it cannot be fully developed in a brief summary such as this. Within a trade union the influence of the left and right wings may be in constant flux. In general, however, union organization has followed the pattern to be outlined.

The first period extends from the immediate postwar confusion to February 1947, when the two great organizations, "Sambetsu Kaigi" (National Congress of Industrial Unions) and "Sodomei" (National Federation of Trade Unions), emerged and stood opposed to each other. During the second period of 1948-1949, which was rather stable, the "Mindo" (Democratic League) made remarkable advances. The third period extends from July 1950 and the formation of "Sohyo" (General Congress of Japanese Trade Unions) to the present. Both "Sodomei" and "Sambetsu Kaigi" were organized about the same time in August 1946, and side by side they shared the role of the big organizer of trade unions in the country. The exact number of unions affiliated with each at the time is not known, but roughly each controlled about half of Japan's organized labor. Meanwhile, "Sambetsu" had come under the influence of leading Communists. Using government and public office employees as a nucleus, they planned the abortive general strike of February 1947, which was banned by order of General Douglas MacArthur, then Supreme Commander for the Allied Powers. This event marked the peak of leftist leadership in Japan's labor movement. It was followed by a re-examination of the Communist leaders and criticism of them by the rank and file members. The organization of the Democratic League within "Sambetsu" in June of 1948 was followed in many unions by a growing repugnance to left-wing leadership. Next came the so-called "Red Purge"—a capitalist offensive with political undertones. The offensive was aimed at clearing the unions of their Communist members and sympathizers, and over 10,000 persons were thus purged by August 1950. Consequently, the labor front underwent a remarkable change. The power of "Sambetsu," which had once been great, began to fade away. This stimulated the growth of such unions as would profess political neutrality. It was at this juncture that "Sohyo" (General Congress of Japanese Trade Unions) planned to regroup the trade unions. Since its formation in July 1950, "Sohyo" has had a steady growth and today claims a membership of 3,500,000, or approximately 60 per cent of the trade union members in the country.

The problems of organization are of the greatest significance to the labor movement, especially in Japan where expansion has been so rapid. In reality, the problem of organization was almost a matter of life or death to Japan's labor movement. The seizure of union leadership was the bone of contention among rival factions, and almost all clashes between rightists and leftists took place over questions of organization. Because Communist and Socialist parties often exerted some influence, the inner workings of trade unions became even more complicated when their affairs became entangled with current issues. At present the majority of unions affiliated with "Sohyo" are friendly to the Left-Wing Socialist Party, while about a half-million members of "Sodomei" support the Right-Wing Socialists. Thus there are clear divisions within the field of organized labor itself. The politically motivated strikes which developed between the summer of 1951 and the spring of 1952 were criticized by the unions' own members. Outside of "Sohyo", there is now an increasingly greater cry for unions to maintain political neutrality.

These 1951–1952 strikes were planned by labor as weapons against the rumored government plan to amend the three basic labor laws—

the Labor Standards Law, the Trade Union Law and the Labor Relations Adjustment Law. The strikes subsequently developed into a fight against the Subversive Activities Prevention Law that was submitted to the Diet. It must be admitted that these strikes, having a political color, played an important part in making the trade union movement throughout the country more politically conscious. In fact, increased activities of trade unions with an expanded political consciousness were among the main causes for the good showing of the Socialist Party in the general election of October 1, 1952. On the other hand, a great deal of public attention is being directed toward the question of how far trade unions should go in their participation in political activities. A careful observer cannot overlook the fact that political activities of trade unions are weakening their activities in the economic field. How these two activities will be integrated into labor policy may well determine the future course of Japanese trade unions.

The three basic labor laws have been amended twice—first in April 1949 and next in August 1952. The first revision had concrete significance because it changed the main objective of the Trade Union Law from a policy that would promote the growth of unions to a policy that would adjust relationships between workers and employers. The second revision had little effect on the substance of the law. Equal in importance to these revisions were the enactment of the National Public Service Law of 1948 and the Public Corporations Labor Relations Law of 1949. These two laws took the right to strike away from public service employees and workers in government-controlled corporations. It is true that these reforms may have been initiated because of actual necessity, but it was unavoidable for trade unions not to interpret the successive readjustments to the laws as planned to restrain their activities which had heretofore been quite free. The unions paid little attention to the reasons offered for the revisions. Each reform, therefore, was met by bitter opposition of the laboring class, which labeled any change a change for the worse. Frankly, it is felt that some of the postwar legislation instituted immediately after the surrender was not consonant with actual conditions in Japan, and there were some instances when the law overshot the mark. As a result, it was inevitable that a certain degree of adjustment to the laws be made as the economy became more stabilized. Judging from early trends, these amendments could be considered reactionary without exception. But we must admit in all fairness that uncontrolled activity on the part of the trade unions was responsible in some measure for having forced the legislators to resort to such measures. It is expected that still further revision of labor legislation will take place according to future developments. Nevertheless, the fundamental principle of democracy which recognizes the legal existence of trade unions today stands quite secure. The trade union has become one of the main pillars of the democratization of Japan. This pillar stands firm and should never be removed.

The trade unions have had bitter experiences in their organizational problems. All the troubles cannot be laid to internal circumstances, however. A good part of their difficulties were encountered in trying to escape from feudalistic practices which were a part of the old system. The unions were also influenced to a remarkable degree by the unstable world situation resulting from the "cold war" between the United States and the Soviet Union. In order to clarify the interrelation of such conditions, let us look at the relationship of Japan's labor movement to the world labor movement.

From an international standpoint, the trend of the Japanese labor movement from the end of the war until 1947 can be summed up as "earliest participation in the World Federation of Trade Unions." The slogan of all labor on May Day in 1946 and 1947 was "Speedy participation in the World Federation of Trade Unions." In 1948, however, this slogan was changed to "Cooperation with the working classes of the world." The change in slogans was, in a way, a criticism directed at the World Federation. The attitude of Japanese workers became clear when the question was raised about Japan's return to the International Labor Organization. For example, when in May 1948, the workers were asked if they wanted Japan to return to the ILO, "Sodomei" immediately answered that it hoped for a return, but "Sambetsu" replied that it placed priority on international unity and that it would be unable to support the plan at that time. The split in the two labor camps thus became clear.

The same question was raised when the time came to decide whether or not to send Japanese observers to the general meeting of the ILO at Geneva in June 1949. "Sambetsu" did not oppose sending representatives, but opposed actual participation in the deliberations. "Sodomei," on the other hand, held that only those who approved of participation were qualified to send delegates. "Sodomei's" point of view prevailed, and delegates were sent from the National Railway Workers Union to be observers at Geneva. After the formation of the International Confederation of Free Trade Unions in September 1949, a lively movement was started, aiming at membership for Japanese unions. With the organization of "Sohyo," the antagonism between "Sambetsu" and "Sodomei" was dissolved. When it was organized in July 1950, "Sohyo" passed a resolution for speedy participation in the ICFTU. However, "Sohyo" itself has not yet entered the organization, although ten " Sohyo " affiliates have elected delegates to the ICFTU and its Asian Area Conference. All such activities reflect the existence of two antagonistic forces in the world, and they indicate the status of the organizational problems of Japan's labor movement today.

In summation, the trade unions of Japan have been faced by the three important problems of wages, contracts and organization. The unions have gradually solidified their position, although they have encountered certain difficulties along the way. Their way of handling problems has varied on occasion, but it may be said that they have generally been following the road of healthy growth and, thereby, attained their present development. The union movement, however, is a reflection of prevailing economic conditions. Only the future will reveal how the trade unions will weather the difficult economic period through which Japan must pass.

POPULATION PROBLEM OF JAPAN

By Ayanori Okazaki

Chief, Institute of Population Problems,
Ministry of Health and Welfare

I. Population Trends During and After World War II

World War II had its inevitable effect on Japan's population. In 1940, the population was 72,300,000, but in 1945 the total had dropped to 72,000,000, a decrease of 300,000. Although the decrease was negligible, it was the first time in the history of Japan since the Meiji Era (1868–1912) that the population total has shown a drop.

Among the many war-time factors contributing to this population decrease were the fall in the marriage rate, the separation of many married couples because of the housing shortage, the drop in the birth rate because of the reduced standard of living, the mass deaths resulting from air-raids, the rise in the natural death rate because of lack of nutrition and reduced medical services and facilities and the dispatch of millions of army and navy servicemen and civilian employees of the military forces to overseas areas.

However, the postwar changes in the population total were more conspicuous than those during the war. In 1950 the population increased sharply to 83,200,000 an increase of 11,200,000, or 15.6 per cent, during the five years from 1945.

The rate of increase during the immediate postwar years was unprecedented. In the 1920–25 period the rate of population increase was 6.9 pre cent; for the 1925–30 period the rate was 8.5 per cent, and in the 1935–40 period it was 7.5 per cent.

II. Analysis of the Postwar Population Increase

A study of the following table of statistics showing the social and natural factors of the period between October 1945 and September 1950 reveals the reasons for the phenomenal population increase in postwar Japan:

(Unit : 1,000)

	Social Factors			Natural Factors			Total In-crease
	Japanese Nationals Repatriated from Overseas Areas	Foreign Nationals Repatriated from Japan	In-crease	Births	Deaths	In-crease	
Oct. 1945— Sept. 1946	4,593	1,038	3,555	1,710	1,520	195	3,745
Oct. 1946— Sept. 1947	1,136	135	1,001	2,644	1,173	1,471	2,472
Oct. 1947— Sept. 1948	329	11	318	2,750	998	1,752	2,070
Oct. 1948— Sept. 1949	156	7	149	2,738	948	1,790	1,939
Oct. 1949— Sept. 1950	34	3	31	2,452	915	1,537	1,568
Total	6,248	1,194	5,054	12,294	5,554	6,740	11,794

The repatriation of Japanese nationals from overseas areas began in October 1945. A total of 5,720,000 Japanese were repatriated in the following two years, and by the end of 1950 the number of re-patriates had risen to 6,250,000. About one-half of the repatriates were ex-servicemen or civilian employees of the Japanese military forces, and this group would have remained as residents of Japan if there had been no war. The remaining half of the Japanese repatri-ates were those who had emigrated to overseas territories and would have continued to live there if Japan had not been defeated.

Foreign nationals, numbering 1,200,000, who had been living in Japan were repatriated to their countries between 1945 and 1950, and they were mostly of Chinese and Korean nationalities.

The exchange of civilian repatriates left Japan with an excess of nearly 2,000,000, which contributed to the social increase in popula-tion.

The natural increase of population in the one year immediately following the end of the war was a mere 190,000. The lack of nutri-tious food during the last stage of the war was the direct cause for the decrease in births and increase in deaths. The birth rate began to show an increase in 1947, while the death rate dropped sharply in 1946 and even more in 1947, in which year there was a marked rise in the rate of natual population increase.

The following table shows the rates of births and deaths against the total population during the postwar years:

TABLE B

	Birth Rate	Death Rate	Natural Increase
1945	24.22%	27.04%	(−) 2.83%
1946	22.45%	19.96%	2.49%
1947	34.30%	14.57%	19.73%
1948	33.43%	11.85%	21.58%
1949	33.17%	11.63%	21.54%
1950	28.33%	10.92%	17.41%
1951	25.60%	10.00%	15.60%
1952	23.60%	9.14%	14.46%

(Note: The birth and death rates for 1952 are estimated on the basis of statistics for the January-May period of that year).

The very low birth rates in 1945 and 1946 noted in the above table are attributable to the intensified air-raids during the last year of the war, conspicuous decrease in conception as a result of the nation-wide social chaos and increased unwillingness of parents to have children because of the extreme social unrest and insecurity prevailing directly after the end of the war.

The death rates during these two years were greatly increased because of the lack of nutrition, shortage of medicine and stagnation of medical activities. The decrease in population because of natural factors in 1945 represents the first time such a drop has occurred in Japan since the beginning of the Meiji Era (1868–1912).

The birth rate increased sharply in 1947 to 34.30 per cent and was 33.17 per cent in 1949, after which it began to drop. The main reasons for the great increase were that millions of soldiers who had been drafted and stationed in Japan proper were demobilized and returned to their homes while other millions of ex-servicemen and overseas residents were repatriated so that in addition to married couples being rejoined the marriage rate increased during the years immediately following the end of the war.

On the other hand, the death rate began to decline sharply in the postwar years. Contributing factors were that the physically weak had died during and immediately after the war, while large quantities of medical supplies were shipped to Japan and the health and sanitary conditions improved. The spectacular drop in the death rate was far beyond expectations.

The increase in the birth rate and decrease in the death rate caused the rate of natural increase to show a remarkable rise. In 1948 and 1949 the natural population increase was 1,700,000 for each year, and the Government and people realized that a serious population problem had once again risen.

III. Propagation and Effect of Birth Control in Postwar Japan

Japan's economy had come to a near standstill at the end of the war, and the conditions of the immediate postwar years reduced economic production capacity. Japan lost about 43 per cent of her territory and, as a result, a very considerable amount of natural resources. Production facilities were extensively damaged or destroyed during the war, and those which had escaped devastation had become superannuated from lack of repair and replacement. Japan's industrial structure was thrown into a state of confusion, and the nation as a whole suffered from almost complete economic paralysis.

Under such circumstances it was only natural that the Japanese people were amenable to any measure which would stop at least temporarily the natural increase of population. In view of this popular desire for controlled parenthood, various independent organizations were established and vigorous campaigns undertaken for the propagation birth control information and methods. Many publications on the subject also became popular, and they frankly explained the principles and methods of birth control which subsequently came to be widely accepted by the people.

Popular demand finally compelled the Ministry of Welfare to authorize in July 1948, the public sale of contraceptives which had hitherto been prohibited. Manufacturers of these contraceptives began a wide sales campaign, and almost daily newspapers and other periodicals carried large-scale advertisements, some of which were unfortunately excessively frank and had undesirable effects on the morals of the younger generation.

As is indicated in Table B, the birth rate climbed sharply in the immediate postwar years until it reached a peak in 1948 and 1949 but showed a definite decline in 1950. It is expected to fall to 23.6 per cent in 1953. The drop in the birth rate is attributable not only to the widespread use of contraceptives but also to the popular practice of abortion. Contraceptives made in Japan were not always of high quality, and conception often occurred where the married couples did not desire parenthood. In such cases, mothers who became pregnant took advantage of the Eugenics Protection Law and often had undergone abortion.

The National Eugenics Law was enacted in 1940 for the purpose of preventing the birth of children being handicapped by hereditary diseases. The Eugenics Protection Law was of a different character and provided not only for the prevention of birth of inferior children from the standpoint of eugenics but also for abortions when they were deemed necessary for the protection and maintenance of the mother's life or health. Article 13 of the Eugenics Protection Law provided that induced abortion was to be authorized in the event that the continued pregnancy or parturitionw as feared to be harmful to the health of the mother on account of physical or economic reasons. The Eugenic Protection Investigation Committee was to study each case before permission for the induced abortion was given under the law. An amendment to the Eugenics Protection Law was enacted and made effective from May 1952, and it became unnecessary for the Eugenics Protection Committee to investigate each case and doctors were authorized to undertake induced abortion on the basis of their own judgement.

In 1949 the cases of induced abortions performed under the Eugenics Protection Law and reported to the Ministry of Welfare numbered 246,104. In 1950 the cases totalled 489,111 and in 1951 there were 636,524. It is estimated that abortion cases would exceed one million in 1953. The ratio of induced abortions to the number of births was 9.1 per cent in 1949 and rose to 28.9 per cent in 1951.

It must be recognized that the statistics of induced abortions given in the preceding paragraph represent only those cases which were reported to the Ministry of Welfare and were undertaken in accordance with the existing law, and it is to be assumed that there were a large number of cases where abortions were undertaken illegally and were not reported to the Ministry of Welfare.

However, induced abortions in many cases had harmful effects on the health of the mothers, and the Ministry of Welfare finally undertook measures to provide better knowledge and methods for preventing conception.

The statistics on the population trends of Japan reveal that the Oriental phenomenon of many births and many deaths has given way to the European practice of few births and few deaths. The decrease in the birth rate has become exceedingly apparent in recent years and is expected to continue in the future as the practice of birth control becomes more popular among the people.

On the basis of estimates of the Institute of Population Problems, the birth rate will be 14.33 per cent and the death rate 10.28 per cent in 1980. Thus, the natural increase will still be somewhat greater than the natural decrease. It is expected, however, that the proportion of aged persons in the composition of the Japanese population will have increased markedly by that time.

The following table compares the 1950 population with the estimated 1980 population on the basis of age groups:

TABLE C

	1950			1980		
	Total	Male	Female	Total	Male	Female
	1,000.0	490.3	509.7	1,000.0	495.6	504.4
4 and under	134.7	68.7	55.0	71.7	36.6	35.1
5-9	114.7	58.1	56.6	71.6	36.5	35.1
10-14	104.7	52.9	51.8	67.4	34.3	33.1
15-19	102.8	51.8	51.0	61.9	31.5	30.4
20-24	92.7	45.9	46.9	68.4	34.8	33.9
25-29	74.1	33.8	40.3	88.0	44.8	43.3
30-34	62.4	28.2	34.1	99.4	50.5	48.9
35-39	60.7	28.5	32.2	85.5	43.2	42.3
40-44	53.9	26.4	27.4	76.7	38.6	38.1
45-49	48.1	24.2	23.8	73.3	36.7	36.6
50-54	40.8	20.7	20.1	64.1	31.4	32.7
55-59	33.0	16.5	16.4	49.2	22.0	27.2
60-64	27.7	13.3	14.4	38.6	16.9	21.7
65-69	21.3	9.6	11.7	33.4	15.0	18.4
70-74	15.5	6.5	9.0	24.3	11.2	13.2
75-79	8.2	3.2	4.9	15.6	7.2	8.5
80 and over	4.5	1.6	3.0	10.8	4.5	6.2

The following illustration shows the above statistics:

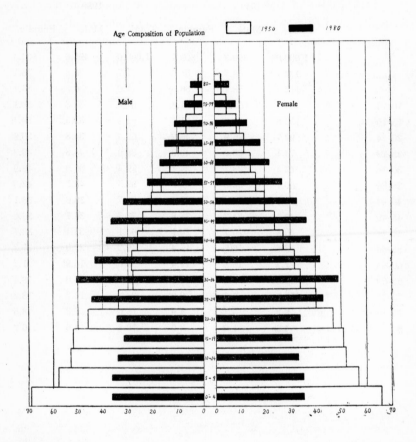

As is indicated in the above illustration, the composition of the population in 1950 by age groups was of a pyramid shape, except that the 25–29 age group was small as a direct result of World War II. In 1980, however, the age groups under 24 years of age, both male and female, will be small, while the middle-age groups will be considerably larger. In the years following 1980 the advanced-age groups will increase further while the younger-age groups will decrease.

IV. Labor and Employment Problem

The objective of restricting the increase of population has been generally achieved thus far. However, the more important aspect of Japan's population problem is the question of employment for the available labor force. The tremendous increase in population in the years immediately following the end of the war was mainly due to the repatriation of overseas Japanese nationals, composed for the most part of young men of the working age group. (The labor population refers to persons between 15 and 59 years of age who have the intention and ability to work but excludes disabled persons, housewives, students and convicts). On the basis of the age composition of the population today, the labor population can be expected to increase in the future.

The following table shows the estimates of the Institute of Population Problems on the character of Japan's labor population from 1950 to 1960:

TABLE D

(Unit: 1,000)

	Total	Male	Female	Total	Male	Female
1950	36,885	22,329	14,556	—	—	—
1951	37,654	22,813	14,841	769	484	285
1952	38,353	23,251	15,102	699	438	261
1953	38,971	23,637	15,334	618	386	232
1954	39,714	24,101	15,613	743	464	279
1955	40,569	24,637	15,932	855	536	319
1956	41,429	25,176	16,253	860	539	321
1957	42,235	25,680	16,555	806	504	302
1958	43,063	26,197	16,866	826	517	311
1959	43,631	26,550	17,081	568	353	215
1960	44,114	26,852	17,262	483	302	181

As indicated in the above table, the labor population is expected to increase from 36,885,000 in 1950 to 44,114,000 in 1960, representing an average increase of about 720,000 a year for the 10 years. Japan is faced with an annual increase in her labor population at approximately this rate provided the ratio of the non-labor population to the labor population remains the same and the death rate does not increase.

The question of providing employment to this growing labor population is a matter of vital importance not only from a social but also from an economic viewpoint. If Japanese industry is unable to provide employment opportunities to the labor population, Japan will be subjected to a continuing social pressure and a deterioration of her economic life.

According to a labor force survey of the Statistics Bureau of the Japanese Government, the labor population of Japan in June 1952, was 39,350,000 and the number of those employed was 38,930,000, leaving 420,000 persons unemployed. This survey revealed that almost 99 per cent of Japan's labor population then had employment. In reality, however, the unemployment situation was far worse than that shown by the statistics.

In prewar years, it was customary in Japan during depression periods for many of the unemployed to be absorbed in the farming industry or retail trade. Thus statistically they did not appear to be unemployed, and unemployment as such was latent. This tendency became conspicuous in postwar years.

Persons employed in the agricultural and forestry industries in June 1952 totalled 18,510,000, according to the labor force survey. The prewar agricultural population was generally constant, totalling 14,130,000 in 1930 and 13,840,000 in 1940. On the basis of the area of existing cultivated areas in Japan and the method of cultivation, a farming population of 14,000,000 is deemed reasonable.

The postwar farming population, however, showed a gradual increase from year to year while the area of cultivated land decreased. Today the farming population has exceeded 18,000,000.

Among the reasons for this increase in the postwar farming population can be listed the following factors:

1. Many of the Japanese nationals repatriated from overseas territories after the end of the war are now living in farming areas.

2. Many of those persons who became unemployed as a result of the wartime devastation of industrial facilities in urban areas have moved to the rural areas.

3. The flow of the excess population in the farming areas to the urban areas has virtually stopped. During the prewar development of Japanese industrial economy, the industries which underwent a remarkable growth under the capitalist system of economy obtained the requisite manpower from the farming areas. In periods when industries suffered from depression, this manpower flowed back to the rural areas and created an economic burden on the farming population. In the final analysis, however, the farming areas benefited under the industrial system since they had a labor market for their excess population.

The industries, which are generally concentrated in the urban areas of Japan, are still weak from the effects of the recent war and are unable to absorb the excess farming population. The result is that the excess labor population is forced to remain in the farming areas.

This characteristic of a latent unemployment situation can also be noted in the conditions of commercial activities. The labor population engaged in commercial activities in June 1952 was 5,390,000, which is considerably greater than the 4,470,000 in 1930, when a serious economic recession resulted in a fairly large number of potentially unemployed persons moving into the commercial field of economic activities. A major reason for this phenomenon was that many unemployed persons were unable to go to the farming areas and remained in the cities by undertaking such occupations as peddlers or street venders. Although the statistics appear to show a favorable trend in the employment situation, latent unemployment is intensified by the unsound distribution of the labor population in the various industries of Japan.

The number of Japanese engaged in the manufacturing industry in June 1952 was 6,310,000, a tremendous drop from the 8,132,000 in 1940 and the wartime peak of 9,131,000 in 1944. The decrease was the result of the closing down of the war industry at the war's end and the delay in building up the peacetime industry.

Many who had lost their jobs in the manufacturing industries poured into agricultural and commercial fields as latently unemployed persons. Moreover, although the number of persons employed in the manufacturing industries has been cut down to approximately 6,300,000, there is danger of a further drastic reduction in the event of an economic depression.

The Government has taken up various plans to meet the problem of excess labor in Japan. In 1947 it established the Emergency Reclamation Program to reclaim 3,800,000 acres of land in 12 years. About 4,000,000 persons were expected to be given employment in the agricultural industry after the reclamation program was completed. However, considerable amounts of funds are required for the program, and no immediate relief is provided for the approximately 4,000,000 excess labor force in the agricultural fields.

Since 1948 the Economic Stabilization Board has been preparing plans for economic rehabilitation and self-sufficiency. These overall plans were intended to build up the economic power of Japan to the 1930–40 level with full consideration being given to the increase in the population. These plans emphasized the development of the manufacturing industry and the expansion of foreign trade. The importance of industrial development and trade promotion is recognized, but the major problems of obtaining capital, including foreign investments, for the development program and of expanding foreign markets for Japanese products remain unsettled.

V. Conclusion

The birth rate in Japan increased sharply in 1947 as ex-servicemen and repatriates came back to rejoin their families or be married after the end of the war, but this rise was of a temporary nature and by 1951 had decreased to the level nearly equal the birth rate in Western countries.

The trend toward fewer births and a lower death rate that has developed in this country will contribute toward a reduced pace of population increase to the benefit, at least temporarily, of a nation suffering from over-population. However, in later years the nation will see a disproportionately large number of persons in the old-age brackets.

The population problem of Japan is so deep-rooted and complicated that the decrease in the birth rate alone will not be a solution. The more important question is how to provide the employment opportunities to the existing and constantly growing population.

Japan has been studying ways to overcome this great problem, and though industrial development and trade expansion are one of the means, international cooperation is a prerequisite.

Once again a member of the comity of free and peace-loving nations, Japan hopes for for such international understanding and cooperation to meet this critical population problem.

ECONOMIC REHABILITATION OF JAPAN AND THE ECONOMY OF ASIA

By Takeshi Yamazaki

Member of the House of Representatives
Former Speaker of the House of Representatives

REHABILITATION

(1) Postwar Japan

More than seven years have passed since the unconditional surrender of Japan in August 1945. The life of the Japanese people
in the days immediately after the end of the Pacific war was miser-
able, particularly in the urban areas. Food, clothing and most daily
necessities were rationed out in amounts far below the even minimum
requirements, and the shortage of staple food was especially distress-
ing. For one full year after the surrender, the food ration to city
dwellers was about 1,000 calories per person a day, according to a
survey by the Bureau of Statistics. This ration supplied less than
one half of the minimum daily requirement of 2,150 calories. In addition, distribution of the staple food ration was usually delayed,
often as long as one month.

Under such circumstances, it seems only natural that almost
everybody was engaged in a frantic scramble to buy food on the
black market at any price.

The Bureau of Statistics has estimated that the average family
at that time spent over 70% of its total budget on food, and out of
the total amount spent in food purchases, some 80% was spent in
the black market. Making allowances for the omissions which are
practically inevitable in any such investigation, it is probably safe
to assume that the amount of money spent on food was much higher
than the Bureau's estimates.

For a while, the people seemed indifferent to shortages in housing and clothing, principally because they were occupied with solving the urgent food problem. Actually, however, housing and clothing shortages were far more acute, as a result of air-raid damage, than superficial examination would indicate. Under the Government plan of 1947, the per capita distribution of clothing was less than one-sixth of the pre-war level, while that of soap was less than one-tenth. Until 1948, practically no improvement was noted in these conditions.

(2) Initiation of Economic Rehabilitation

When economic conditions showed a degree of improvement in 1948, the Japanese Government prepared a five-year recovery program scheduled to begin in 1949, with the goal of raising production to 130% of the pre-war level, and thereby elevating the standard of living to 90% of the pre-war level.

It was then believed that economic recovery of all Asia was an essential condition to the success of the Japanese program, which was indeed based on the principle that the economy of Japan should be integrated into the world economy.

Japan lost almost one-half of her entire territory as a result of the defeat, and in the remaining area, some eighty million persons including repatriates from her former overseas possessions, had to be fed. In addition, the peopulation of Japan continued to increase at the annual rate of 1.5%.

The authors of the economic recovery program believed that in order to provide employment and an adequate standard of living for the Japanese people, it would be necessary to expand the export program and at the same time, promote imports of commodities which would contribute to the production of export goods. The main reason for their arriving at this conclusion was their belief that domestic natural resources had been developed to the limit.

Because Japan's major export markets and sources of raw material and food imports have traditionally been in Asia, the economic planners thought that Japan's economic recovery would depend on the recovery of those Asian nations. Unless those nations recovered, they would be unable either to import Japanese merchandise or to produce export goods.

(3) Actual Progress toward Rehabilitation

The economy of Japan has already surpassed the goals of the 1949 five-year plan, with respect both to production and living standards.

Average annual income is now approximately $150 per capita, which, although low in comparison with average incomes in America and western Europe, is considerably higher than that of any other country in Asia.

Compared to the desperate conditions of a few years ago, the speed of Japan's economic rehabilitation is nothing less than amazing, especially if the tremendous losses suffered in the war are considered.

Noteworthy in this connection, however, is the fact that Japan's recovery did not result from sound development in concert with the economic recovery and development of other Asian nations, as envisaged in the original plan.

It is true that some Asian countries have made remarkable economic progress, but in some, political instability still hinders development. Japan's trade with Southeast Asian nations has increased each year, but not to the extent which we might desire. Still, Japan's economic recovery has been proceeding with great speed.

The answer to this phenomenon undoubtedly lies in the Korean conflict, which brought to Japan an unexpected windfall of dollars.

This, however, cannot be regarded as economically sound, with the prosperity of the nation depending on such a situation.

The economy of Japan, which had appeared to be making favorable progress until 1951, actually suffered reverses in 1952, with the decline of the export-import trade. This fact indicates clearly that in order to develop the Japanese economy soundly, Japan must try to promote economic relations with peaceful Asian nations, and to build prosperity not on the misfortunes of Japan's neighbors, but on their happiness.

ASIAN ECONOMY AND JAPAN

Rational economic development of Japan should be based on close trade relations with Asian countries. The following table shows Asia's share in Japan's foreign trade, in relation to the rest of the world.

1934—1936

	Export	Import
Asia	64%	53%
Neighboring Countries	(44)	(37)
Southeast Asian Countries	(17)	(16)
North America	17	25
Others	19	22
Total	100	100

1951

	Export	Import
Asia	51%	28%
Neighboring Countries	(9)	(4)
Southeast Asian Countries	(36)	(20)
North America	16	46
Others	33	26
Total	100	100

As the table shows, before the war, Asia accounted for 64% of Japan's exports and 53% of imports, unquestionably an important share of Japanese foreign commerce. At the time, of course, Korea and Formosa were Japanese colonies, and much of China was within Japan's sphere of economic influence.

From China, Japan formerly imported iron ore, coking coal, salt, soya beans and oil seeds; from Formosa, rice and sugar; from Korea, rice; from Manchuria, soya beans; and from Southeast Asia, iron ore, rubber, bauxite, raw cotton, copra, non-ferrous metals, etc.

Principal imports from other areas included wool from Australia, raw cotton from the United States, and steel, scrap iron and machinery from the United States and Europe.

Japan exported cotton cloth and miscellaneous goods to Southeast Asia, and such heavy industrial products as machinery and rolling stock to Korea, Manchuria and China, in addition to textiles and fiber products.

The products exchanged in this commerce were significant from the standpoint of not only quantity but also quality. The Asian nations provided foodstuffs and essential raw materials to Japan and imported from Japan heavy industrial products and cotton cloth. Also noteworthy is the fact that this trade always showed an excess of exports from Japan over imports.

By contrast, in trade with the United States—another important element in Japan's foreign commerce—the balance was unfavorable, with imports far exceeding exports to America, because of importation of great quantities of raw cotton, particularly since 1932.

An excess of exports to Southeast Asia compensated for this unfavorable balance of trade, thus giving Asia three-fold significance in the pre-war picture of Japan's foreign trade. Trade with Asia was characterized by large volume and based on exports of Japan's staple products, and, as a result of the excess of exports over imports, it compensated for unfavorable trade with other areas.

But what is the postwar situation? If there has been any change, what is its significance to the economy of Japan?

Consideration of the circumstances surrounding trade in four items—rice, iron ore, cotton cloth and machinery—which constitute the most important commodities in commerce between Japan and other Asian nations, will furnish some clues to the answer.

(1)　Rice

In order to obtain sufficient food, Japan must import from 3 to 3.5 million tons of staple food each year. Before the war, Japan was able to obtain almost enough rice from Korea and Formosa to make up for the shortage of rice in Japan proper. Loss of these sources of food as a result of the war had a most serious impact on Japan's economy. Even though rice production might be restored in those areas, there is little prospect that Japan could expect to import rice as in the days when Korea and Formosa were Japanese colonies.

Consequently, Japan now directs her attention to Southeast Asia as a potential source of food supplies. These Southeast Asian nations —Indo-China, Thailand and Burma—produced about 12 million tons of polished rice annually before the war, and exported approximately 6 million tons each year, chiefly to India, Malaya, Ceylon and other Southeast Asian countries. Japan purchased Southeast Asian rice only in exceptional instances, such as when crops failed in areas which usually provided her supply.

After the war, Japan has been able to import only about 500,000 tons annually from Southeast Asia, and obliged to import wheat and rice from the United States, Canada, Australia and other areas. This contributed to the maintenance of an unfavorable "dollar balance" in Japan's foreign trade.

Southeast Asia's rice export capacity is limited at present because in Burma and Indo-China, production has barely attained 70% of the pre-war average. In addition, domestic food consumption is rising as a result of population increase in that area.

Some Southeast Asian nations are building their economic development programs around increased food production, and food production in India and the Philippines actually exceeds the pre-war figures.

If food production in Burma and Indo-China continues at the present level, however, the area's rice export capacity may diminish as population increases, even after the present development plans are completed.

On the other hand, it is extremely important for Japan to import more food from Southeast Asia in order to reduce the burden of dollar area imports. To attain this objective, it will be essential that food production be increased not only in such food-exporting countries as Burma and Indo-China, but also in the food-importing countries of Southeast Asia.

Needless to point out, Japan cannot expect to fill all her needs in this area, but if as much as 1.5 million tons of rice could be imported, it would represent a tremendous improvement over the present situation.

(2) Iron Ore

Japan's principal problem in this regard is how to obtain sufficient supplies of iron ore and coking coal. Before the war, Southeast Asia was an important source of iron ore for Japan, in contrast to the pre-war rice situation. About one-half of Japan's total imports of iron ore came from Malaya and the Philippines. At the outbreak of the Pacific War, China became an important supplier, shipping more than 4 million tons to Japan in 1942.

China, however, is not rich in iron resources, and with the exception of the Anshan area, the only mines of any importance are poor ones, located at Tayeh on the Yangtse River, Lungyen in Mongolia, and Shihlu on Hainan Island.

If a large-scale iron industry is ever established in China, it will become apparent that her ore resources relatively speaking are not abundant. On the contrary, Southeast Asia has fairly rich iron mines in Orissa and Bihar in India, Srigao and Costi in Goa, Samar in the Philippines, and Dungun in Malaya.

During 1951, Japan imported about 4 million tons of iron ore, abou half of which came from Southeast Asia. In that year, Japan's steel production reached 4.3 million tons. In order to raise annual production to the hoped-for minimum goal of 5 million tons, Japan will have to import 7 million tons of ore, for domestic supplies hardly amount to one million tons. If the Southeast Asian mines can be fully developed, they will be able to produce more iron ore than Japan's needs. This would eliminate the necessity of importing iron ore from the United States, which now amounts to about half the total purchased abroad by Japan, and would thereby reduce Japan's dollar expenditures. In addition, such a development would probably have the effect of placing Japan's steel industry in a better competitive position, by making possible lower prices.

Coal deposits in Japan are comparatively poor, as in the case of iron ore, and good coking coal in particular, is extremely scarce. It is therefore necessary that Japan import much coking coal from other countries. Before the war, practically all the coking coal imported by Japan came from China. Outside of China, other Asian sources of coking coal are India and Indonesia, although Indonesia's coking coal is not of the best quality.

As long as Japan's trade with China is suspended, Japan will have to depend on America for necessary raw materials, although the iron and steel industry of Japan has been historically based and developed on the premise that raw materials would be easily available from nearby countries. The severance of trade relations between Japan and the China mainland, as a result, hinders the development of the Japanese iron and steel industry.

(3) Cotton Cloth

Of the total value of Japanese exports, almost one half is represented by fiber products, half of which in turn consists of cotton cloth. About 50% of all cotton cloth exports go to Southeast Asia.

From the beginning of the Showa period, about 28 years ago, Japan's exports showed a remarkable increase, principally because of exports of cotton cloth to Southeast Asia.

At present, however, although Japan has nearly 7 million spindles, capable of producing 2 billion yards of cotton cloth for export each year, actual exports amount to less than 1 billion yards. The pre-war peak for cotton cloth exports was 2.7 billion yards.

One major reason for the decline in cotton cloth exports is the fact that Asian countries are developing their own cotton textile industries. India, which was the biggest pre-war market for Japanese cotton cloth, and once imported 600 million yards in one year, now imports no cotton cloth, and instead is exporting some one billion yards annually.

Pakistan has replaced the former Indian market to some degree, however, and imports about 250 million yards a year. But at the same time, Pakistan, which produces raw cotton, is exhibiting a tendency to develop her own cotton textile industry, and if the Colombo Plan is carried out, Pakistan will not have to import any cotton cloth.

Although other Southeast Asian countries may not at present be in a position to reduce imports, they are intent upon increasing their domestic cotton textile production capacity.

Actual consumption of cotton products per capita in Southeast Asia is about one-half the average individual consumption throughout the world. It is therefore probable that if income levels in Southeast Asia rise, the demand for clothing will gradually increase, and despite the development of domestic production facilities, Japan would be able to export even more cotton goods to those nations than at present.

On the other hand, it is possible that if Japan, as the self-designated "Factory of Asia", were to export great quantities of cotton cloth to Southeast Asia, the industrialization of those nations would be adversely affected, and it would become apparent that such a policy would hinder the economic development of Asia in general.

It seems inadvisable for Japan to attempt to rebuild her traditional economic ties with other Asian nations on the basis of cotton cloth exports, as in pre-war days.

(4) Machinery

Although the pre-war overseas market for Japanese machines was practically limited to Manchuria and China, the post-war market for such merchandise now includes Southeast Asia, in keeping with the recent tendency toward industrialization of that area.

Principal export items comprise spinning and weaving machines to India and Pakistan, rolling stock to Thailand, bicycles to Indonesia and internal-combustion engines to India.

The ratio of machinery to all exports to Southeast Asia has risen from less than 5% before the war to 11% in 1951. The total amount of these exports is not high, however, and by 1952, was still less than $50 million.

Japan's production capacity for such items as tractors, bulldozers, trucks, mining and engineering machinery, ships, electric machines and vehicles can be expanded beyond present levels, and economic development of Southeast Asia will create an increased demand for these products.

But the Southeast Asian economic development programs have not all made rapid progress, usually because of lack of capital, and Japanese machinery must compete in the export market with European and American products. Japan's machine industry is faced with the fact that it is inferior in some points to American and European machine industries, while it is handicapped by the necessity of using high-priced steel raw materials.

It is obvious, however, that with the progress of Southeast Asian nations toward self-sufficiency in the production of fiber goods and miscellaneous items, Japan should place major emphasis on the development of export trade in machinery.

CONCLUSION

The pre-war overseas trade of Japan with Asian nations had three outstanding features: (1) large volume, (2) relative importance of certain types of merchandise, and (3) the fact that trade with Asian countries was a key factor in enabling Japan to settle her international accounts.

At present, the volume of trade with Asian nations has become lower, in comparison to trade with other areas. It is especially noteworthy that while the volume of trade with nearby countries in Asia has decreased sharply, that with Southeast Asia has risen. Trade with neighboring countries has dropped mainly as a result of the loss of the former colonies of Korea and Formosa, removal of Manchuria from Japan's sphere of influence, and Communist domination of mainland China. Southeast Asia's economic development has led to an increased demand for Japanese products in that area, which has now become the pivot of Japanese overseas trade with Asian nations. But because trade with neighboring areas has not recovered, Asia's share of Japan's aggregate foreign trade is still far below the pre-war level.

As for the second outstanding feature, although the composition of exports and imports is generally the same as in pre-war years, a number of significant changes have occurred on some points. In exports, the importance of cloth has diminished considerably, while the relative importance of machinery has risen steadily. This trend may be expected to become more marked in the future.

With regard to imports, the most striking change has taken place in rice, which was formerly imported in large quantities from Korea and Formosa, but which now comes, though in inadequate amounts, from Southeast Asia.

Iron ore, which formerly came from China, now is imported from Southeast Asia, and for coal, Japan must now depend on America. Although in prewar days, India was the source of an enormous quantity of raw cotton for Japan, such is no longer the case, and no raw cotton is imported from that country.

The principal cause for these changes is the suspension of trade with neighboring countries, coupled with the growing tendency toward industrialization of various Asian nations.

The third major characteristic of Japan's pre-war Asian commerce has also undergone great change. Before the war Japan's unfavorable trade balances with some countries were compensated for by favorable balances with others.

As a result of existing restrictions on currency exchange, however, it is now impossible to achieve such equilibrium. Japan imports from the United States foodstuffs, raw cotton, iron ore and coal, thereby incurring enormous dollar debits, but is unable to use earnings from exports to Southeast Asia to pay her debts to the United States. No matter how much Japan exports to the Southeast Asian area, she cannot purchase from other currency areas merchandise of equivalent value.

Although this situation retards development of Japanese commerce with Southeast Asia, it paradoxically enhances the importance of the Asian market to the economy of Japan. Japan has an unfavorable balance of about $800 million annually in her trade with the dollar area. Although this deficit is covered by current dollar receipts accruing from special procurement orders and the like, this situation can be regarded as only temporary, and once such dollars cease to flow in, Japan will be forced to purchase at least some necessary raw materials and foodstuffs from Asian countries.

Japan's economic relationship to the new Asia is no longer that of an industrial nation to a group of colonies. Regardless of whatever food or raw materials Japan may want, or whatever market she may seek for her machinery or chemical fertilizer, she will be unable to increase the volume of her trade, unless the economy of the various Asian nations is further developed.

Awareness of these facts accounts for Japan's present attitude on international trade relations, and also for her unceasing efforts toward assisting in the economic development of Southeast Asia. Examples of these efforts may be found in the proposed construction of a blast furnace at Orissa, India, erection of a magnesium-clinker plant at Madras and development of iron mines in Goa and salt fields in Thailand, although these projects have not yet been fully materialized.

There are, however, still many problems, the satisfactory solution of which will be no easy task. For instance, Japan's failure to restore economic relations with neighboring nations, and slow progress in the economic development of some Southeast Asian nations, as a result of political instability and capital shortages, contribute to delaying economic rehabilitation of the entire area.

In addition, present restrictions on currency exchange make it necessary for Japan to balance her accounts with each nation individually, rather than employ a system of multilateral settlement. Western nations will undoubtedly compete vigorously with Japan for Asian markets, and it is quite possible that Japan's economic activities in those Asian nations will create suspicion as to her motives.

Economic relationships include not only elements of mutual existence and mutual prosperity, but also conflict of interests. At the present time, Japan's economic relations with Asian nations are fundamentally not competitive but complementary.

The economy of Japan, in order to develop in a sound manner, must inevitably be based on the assumption that the progress of her neighbors toward wealth and prosperity is an important factor in her own prosperity.